Basics of Bible Interpretation

A *Discovery Bible Study Book*

Basics of Bible Interpretation

Bob Smith

WORD BOOKS
PUBLISHER
4800 WEST WACO DRIVE
WACO, TEXAS
76703

Contents

Introduction

Acknowledgments

PHASE 1: BACK TO BASICS

For everyone who wants to understand what God has said to man in his Word.

PHASE 2: FIGURATIVE LANGUAGE

A look at the fascinating world of metaphoric and symbolic language.

PHASE 3: BIBLICAL LANGUAGES

A bit of insight into the thought patterns of the Hebrew and Greek language behind our English text.

PHASE 4: STRUCTURAL ANALYSIS

The final step: analyzing structure and summarizing in outline form.

A constant source of encouragement to me and to many others has been the example of my dear friend and compatriot, *Bob Roe*. His diligent, careful study of God's Word, his obedient response to its truth, and his able teaching ministry which is the result, are a challenge to anyone who sees the possibility of being taught by God. Without formal theological training, he rates in my book as able apologist, thorough theologian, compassionate pastor and all-around man of God. I'm glad he's also my friend. I dedicate this book to him. May his tribe increase.

Introduction

I hope that this book will meet a need. Many of God's people have expressed to me that they do not have a handle on how to approach the Bible to become good, accurate interpreters of its contents.

There are seminary courses on hermeneutics (the art of Bible interpretation) and books on the subject, but the courses are out of reach for most and the books are often too voluminous and imposing to invite reading. Yet I believe that God wants all of us to be able to study the Bible intelligently and understand its message . . . hence this book.

I have a thing about thick books and big words, so if you're expecting an exhaustive (and exhausting) tome, replete with all the theological jargon, you'll be disappointed. This is not a scholarly treatise with a high fog rating. As did Paul the apostle, I want to use great plainness of speech, for no one should be excluded from the profitable and exciting possibility of discovering the truth of God through his own independent study of the Bible.

I have tried to assume as little as possible on the part of the reader, so some of the material is on a rather elementary level. If it seems too basic, remember that every year football teams go back to the basics of blocking, tackling, running,

kicking, and passing—so reviewing the basics of Bible interpretation is not altogether bad. I believe you may find plenty
to challenge your thinking, however, even if you are already
somewhat skilled in interpreting the Scriptures.

This is a study book. If you do not have your Bible side-by-
side with it as you study you will miss much of its value. The
format I have used is simple. I have cited principles by which
one can interpret the Scriptures, then I have illustrated the
use of those principles to analyze a portion of scripture. You
will want to follow my analysis step by step in your own Bible
to really appreciate what I'm trying to do. You may not agree
with all of my interpretive opinions, but I hope you will have
gained the capability of reaching your own conclusions based
on your personal application of interpretive principles.

The theme song you should be singing throughout is:
"Man shall not live by bread alone, but by every word
   that proceeds from the mouth of God" (Matt. 4:4).
God has spoken! His are words to live by! So we must seek to
understand the *Basics of Bible Interpretation*.

Acknowledgments

While I will attempt to acknowledge sources where possible, I'm sure I have borrowed much from many faithful teachers and authors whose material I have absorbed over the years so that they seem like my own. I am especially indebted to Milton S. Terry's *Biblical Hermeneutics,* a comprehensive treatment typical of the careful scholarship of the nineteenth century. I marvel that anyone had the time and scholarly persistence to produce such a thoroughly documented and illustrated volume. I'm also amazed I got through its 782 pages! This book won't be half that hard, but I hope it will be at least half as helpful.

I owe so much to so many, I hardly know where to start and where to stop in acknowledgment of my indebtedness. But I must say "thanks" to many of my fellow-workers for their help in the preparation of this book, to those whose kindly critiques have been so valuable: Bob Roe, Dick and Judy Grant, Jim Blain, David Roper, Ron Ritchie, Steve Newman, Bev Blake, Patrick Cunningham, Carleen Brooks, Jean McAllister, Paul Winslow, Steve and Erica Lawry.

Special thanks are due David Roper for his contribution on Old Testament Hebrew and his study questions on 2 Timothy. Then, last but far from least, there is the labor of love represented in the multiple typings and retypings by Dottie Canoose. Thanks, Dottie.

It's always a special joy to work with our son, Dave Smith, on the art work for my books. I like the father/son act. Besides, it means he has to read what his "ole dad" writes, and I love to share the great truth God has given us with him and all our loved ones.

Phase 1

Back to

Basics

□ 1 □

Words of Life

God wants everyone to be able to understand the Bible, for its message is essentially how we can have and enjoy the greatest kind of life, free from the futility of pointlessness, free from the limitations of our human, earthly thought patterns, free from the fear of death and dying.

Not everyone understands it this way. In fact, many are so convinced they can't understand the Bible that they never give it a second look. It's strange how we will study most any other subject with diligence only to have the acquired knowledge perish with us. But the words of the Bible are words of life!

> . . . I have set before you *life* and death, blessing and cursing; therefore choose life, that you and your descendants may *live,* loving the Lord your God, obeying his voice, and cleaving to him; for that means *life* to you . . . (Deut. 30:19, 20, italics mine).

Even here in the Old Testament, which many think offers only wrath, God plainly wants us to choose *life.* And there are many similar expressions in the Old Testament:

> Thou dost show me the path of
> life. . . (Ps. 16:11).

. . . the Lord has commanded
the blessing,
life for evermore (Ps. 133:3).

Thy commandment makes me wiser
than my enemies,
for it is ever with me.
I have more understanding than all
my teachers,
for thy testimonies are my meditation.
I understand more than the aged,
for I keep thy precepts.
I hold back my feet from every evil
way,
in order to keep thy word.

I rejoice at thy word
like one who finds great spoil. (Ps 119:98–101, 162).

The fear of the Lord leads to life:
and he who has it rests satisfied . . . (Prov. 19:23).

Then there is Isaiah's word:

For as the rain and the snow come
down from heaven,
and return not thither but water
the earth,
making it bring forth and sprout,
giving seed to the sower and bread
to the eater,
so shall my word be that goes forth
from my mouth;
it shall not return to me empty,
but it shall accomplish that which I
purpose,
and prosper in the thing for which
I sent it.
For you shall go out in joy,
and be led forth in peace . . . (Isa. 55:10–12).

Notice, in the same way God blesses man with rain and snow —to feed him and sustain his life—so he also sends forth his word. His purpose is that we may have joy and peace (v. 12). As one might expect, the New Testament overflows with the same thought. Listen to the words of the Lord Jesus:

> Truly, truly, I say to you, he who hears my word and believes him who sent me, has eternal life; he does not come into judgment, but has passed from death to life (John 5:24).
>
> . . . the words that I have spoken to you are spirit and life (John 6:63).
>
> . . . I came that they may have life, and have it abundantly (John 10:10).

The rest of the New Testament uses terms like: "holding fast the word of life" (Phil. 2:16) and ". . . the word of his grace which is able to build you up and to give you the inheritance . . ." (Acts 20:32). Peter calls it "the living and abiding word of God" (1 Peter 1:23).

The writer of Hebrews tells us: ". . . the word of God is living and active, sharper than any two-edged sword, piercing to the division of soul and spirit . . . and discerning the thoughts and intentions of the heart" (Heb. 4:12).

So we seem to have ample evidence from the Bible itself that it is eminently worthwhile for us to read and understand the Bible. From the Scriptures we have cited, we could even put it stronger: it is really a "life and death" matter.

God's Problem

But God had a problem. Since he is obviously bigger than both of us—infinite, eternal and utterly unchanging—he could find it difficult to communicate with the likes of us who live on an entirely different plane. As Isaiah puts it, speaking for the Lord,

For just as the heavens are higher than the earth so are my ways higher than yours, and my thoughts than yours (Isa. 55:9, Living Bible).

Yet God was so concerned that we know the beauty of his plan and the surpassing scope of his love for us that he broke through the communication barrier. He took the trouble to put his thoughts toward us in a book, so we can know what life is all about, in time and eternity. But more than that, we can know him, this God who cares about us. His communication went even further: He sent his personal emissary, his Son, to show us what he is like and what we should be like. So we have both a written and a personal revelation.

In many and various ways God spoke of old to our fathers by the prophets; *but in these last days he has spoken to us by a Son,* whom he appointed the heir of all things, through whom also he created the world. He reflects the glory of God and bears the very stamp of his nature . . . (Heb. 1:1–3, italics mine).

First we are told, "God spoke in many and various ways by the prophets . . . ." Multi-media communication we call it today. Then the Bible tells us he sent his Son, a living, walking, talking, loving demonstration of his own nature, in three-dimensional, living color. He really wants us to understand and know him! I suspect that no one has ever taken such initiative and such care to be understood.

His Book tells us more. It says: In the beginning was the Word, and the Word was with God, and the Word was God . . . and the Word became flesh and dwelt among us, full of grace and truth . . . (John 1:1 and 14).

He even called his Son "the Word" (and, I might add, the *last* word) so concerned is he about communication with man —for "No one has ever seen God; the only Son, who is in the bosom of the Father, he has made him known" (John 1:18).

God records the life and love of the *Living* Word, the Lord Jesus, in his Book in *written* words. The concern of God's heart to reveal himself to us is beautifully expressed by the apostle Paul in these words:

> . . . we speak God's wisdom in a mystery, the hidden wisdom, which God predestined before the ages to our glory; the wisdom which none of the rulers of this age has understood; for if they had understood it, they would not have crucified the Lord of glory; but just as it is written,
> "Things which eye has not seen and ear has
>   not heard,
> And which have not entered the heart of man,
> All that God has prepared for those who love
>   Him."
>
> *For to us God revealed them* through the Spirit; for the Spirit searches all things, even the depths of God. For who among men knows the thoughts of a man except the spirit of the man, which is in him? Even so the thoughts of God no one knows except the Spirit of God. Now we have received, not the spirit of the world, but the Spirit who is from God, *that we might know the things freely given to us by God,* which things we also speak, *not in words taught by human wisdom, but in those taught by the Spirit,* combining spiritual thoughts with spiritual words (1 Cor. 2:7–13 NASV, italics mine).

Did you catch the import of that?

⊤ What man could not understand through his eyes, or ears, or heart, God has *revealed* to us. Some *revelation,* I'd say! Just what I always wanted to know, but could never find out. But that's not all.

⊤ We have received the Spirit who is from God—*that we might know* the things God has freely given us. God sent us a private tutor to teach us of his good gifts so we might enjoy them. That's *illumination.* How good can it get? But that's still not all.

⊤ He communicated in *words* taught by the Spirit, matching up spiritual concepts with spiritual words! That's *inspiration.* He took man's words, used human writers and speakers with all their fallibility and frailty, to say exactly what he wants us to know—in human language.

And what did he say? Well, you'll have to read his Book to get it all, but primarily he wants us to know that he loves us and is available to live our lives with us and in us to make life great—in time and eternity. But he doesn't kid us about the real problems and difficulties we'll face either. He just tells us the truth.

How does he say it? He isn't stuck with limited imagination and creativity as we often are, so he uses all of the various and varied means of communication available in human language. He uses straight-from-the-shoulder talk like logical, reasoning discourse; commands as to exactly what we must do; real-life stories about real people; as well as less direct but equally effective teaching through parables, figures of speech, poetry, songs, history, intrigue, prophecy, and all kinds of blood-and-thunder stories.

But in all of its various moods and modes of expression he tells us the truth about himself—and about us.

□ 2 □

Is Anybody Listening?

God still has a problem. It's this: Is anyone really listening? Most everyone (in the Western world, at least) has access to a copy of his Book, but not everyone reads it and understands it. As a matter of fact, though there are parts of the Bible that anyone can understand, no one understands all of it. But God is only concerned that we keep listening and learning so he can communicate to us what we need to know when we need to know it. He is so lovingly practical that he doesn't want to burden our minds and hearts with a lot of academic, unlived truth. He just wants to keep equipping us for all we face in life. So there's no graduation from this course of study—it's a lifetime curriculum.

It's also a tough curriculum. It's not easy to understand God's Book. He has things to say that are beyond the realm of our experience, so no wonder it's difficult. But the Lord says repeatedly, "He who has an ear to hear, let him hear." Since he made us with two ears, he's not questioning our anatomy, only whether we're really listening and responding to his Word.

He knows that his are words to live by, for he said, "Man shall not live by bread alone, but by every word that proceeds from the mouth of God" (Matt. 4:4 and Deut. 8:3). Our

Lord Jesus Christ lived by the vital truth of God's Word. His life was a pattern of obedience to God's Word and he was ever quoting it and teaching it as the word of truth. He said to the Father, "Thy word is truth" (John 17:17b).

Regarding the Old Testament scriptures he said, "Blessed rather are those who hear the word of God and keep it" (Luke 11:28). And to proud Pharisees he said, "You have a fine way of rejecting the commandment of God, in order to keep your tradition . . . thus making void the word of God . . ." (Mark 7:9, 13).

He attested to the Old Testament record concerning Adam and Eve, Moses, and Jonah. He attested to the unchanging truth of "the law and the prophets" (a term for the Old Testament Scriptures) with complete confidence in their credibility and reliability as the Word of God.

⊤ He speaks concerning Adam and Eve:

He answered, "Have you not read that he who made them from the beginning made them male and female, and said, 'For this reason a man shall leave his father and mother and be joined to his wife, and the two shall become one flesh?' " (Matt. 19:4, 5).

Here he quotes from Genesis 1 and 2, the creation story, treating it as authoritative.

⊤ He has confidence in Moses' writings, and the prophets:

And beginning with Moses and all the prophets, he interpreted to them in all the scriptures the things concerning himself (Luke 24:27).

⊤ He quotes the Psalms and prophets:

"I am not speaking of you all; I know whom I have chosen; it is that the scripture may be fulfilled, 'He who ate my bread has lifted his heel against me' " (John 13:18, a quotation from Ps. 41:9).

. . . and there was given to him the book of the prophet Isaiah. He opened the book and found the place where it was written, "The Spirit of the Lord is upon me, because he has anointed me to preach good news to the poor. He has sent me to proclaim release to the captives and recovering of sight to the blind, to set at liberty those who are oppressed, to proclaim the acceptable year of the Lord" (Luke 4:17–19, a quotation from Isa. 61:1–2).

And he began to say to them, "Today this scripture has been fulfilled in your hearing" (Luke 4:21).

⊤ He insists on the authority and permanence of the Old Testament scriptures:

Do not think that I came to abolish the Law or the Prophets; I did not come to abolish, but to fulfill. For truly I say to you, until heaven and earth pass away, not the smallest letter or stroke shall pass away from the Law, until all is accomplished (Matt. 5:17, 18 NASV).

⊤ He claims to speak for God in his earthly ministry:

. . . The words that I say to you I do not speak on My own initiative, but the Father abiding in Me does His works. . . . He who does not love Me does not keep My words: and the word which you hear is not Mine, but the Father's who sent Me (John 14:10, 24 NASV).

⊤ He gives warrant for New Testament revelation:

These things I have spoken to you, while I am still with you. But the Counselor, the Holy Spirit, whom the Father will send in my name, he will teach you all things, and bring to your remembrance all that I have said to you. . . . But when the Counselor comes, whom I shall send to you from the Father, even the Spirit of truth, who proceeds from the Father, he will bear witness to me; and you also are witnesses, because you have been with me from the beginning. . . . I have yet many things to say to you, but you cannot bear them now. When the Spirit of truth comes, he will guide you into all the truth; for he will not speak on his own authority, but whatever he hears he will speak and he will declare to you the things that are to come. He will glorify me, for he will take what is mine and declare it to you (John 14:25, 26, 15:26, 27; and 16:12–14).

After all, we who are called by his name should take no other view than that of Jesus Christ, our Lord.

That means we must listen to God's word—with both ears.

The Attitude That Promotes Understanding

But how do we make sure we're getting it straight? I can't tell you how many times I've heard the objection, "There are so many interpretations of the Bible I don't think we can be sure of what it means. So why study it?" My usual reply is to ask the objector to interpret a verse like John 3:16. He usually finds he *can* understand it. Hopefully, this approach will get people started.

I hope differences of interpretive opinion don't deter *you,* for there is a simple explanation for them. It is this: we all have limited understanding of the truth, so our areas of ignorance can easily explain our lack of agreement. After all, scientists often disagree in their interpretation of the physical world, but this only spurs their interest and stimulates them to deeper study.

Regarding the Scriptures, through the apostle Paul, God testifies of *all* of us, "Now I know in part" (1 Cor. 13:12b). So we, like many scientists do, should take the humble place of the *learner,* for a lifetime. The most important issue is the attitude with which we approach the Scriptures.

The Book That Goes with Man

As we view man, we see that he is unique. He is uniquely capable of thinking and reasoning. When I talk to some of my scientific friends, I marvel at their ability to think in abstract, unseen, and unseeable realms of investigation. When I hear a great symphony orchestra, I am amazed at the ability of the composer and the orchestra to create and execute such a masterpiece of sound and rhythm which can profoundly move my feelings and responses. These marvelous talents are God-given and unique to the human species.

Turning to the Bible, I am equally amazed at its richness of expression of the great themes of the grace and mercy of God extended to us because he loves us. I am amazed by the honesty with which he tells us the truth about ourselves even when it hurts, and then assures us of his redemptive answer to the hurt. The clarity with which the Scriptures see what I'm like suggests that its authors must be reading my mail or my mind—or else, the ultimate Author must be the one who made me and knows me through and through.

This knowledge could be deadly, and totally unwelcome, if God were not concerned about my ultimate good through it all. But since he is concerned about my well-being, it seems to me I can handle anything God has to say to me.

So ours should be an attitude of openness and expectancy when we study the Bible. If we examine the finished products, man and God's Book as they exist, we come to the conclusion that they correlate, and the Bible is the Book that goes with man. For the truth of the Bible speaks so clearly and forcefully to·the crucial issues of life that the correlation is unmistakable.

I don't want myself, or you, to be naive and gullible in these matters, but neither do I want to be like a stubborn, unreasoning donkey. A teachable spirit is a joy to see—in mules or in men. The Bible talks about the "simplicity that is in Christ" (2 Cor. 11:3 KJV). The word in the Greek text for "simplicity" means mental honesty, or openness of heart. This attitude of approach to the Scriptures is not simplistic, but rather it leads to the discovery of the most profound truth —truth that applies to life.

Understanding Language

The use of language for communication is uniquely a faculty of man. As early in the Bible as the second chapter of Genesis, God instructed Adam to name the animals. Thus it seems basic to man's nature to use language to express what he sees and feels.

It would appear that the earlier forms of writing were in pictographs, in which the written character pictured, in stylized fashion, the object observed. The development of more sophisticated expression through alphabets, words, grammatical usage, and the various parts of speech is virtually untraceable. It seems, though, that communication through spoken or written symbols is inherent in man.

Communicating through Symbols

Languages are basically symbolic, whether spoken or written, and if one does not have an understanding of how the symbols are employed to communicate thoughts and concepts, there is no communication. If you have ever visited a foreign country where you did not understand the language, this fact comes home to you with a bit of a shock. All communication in human language is based on a common understanding of the symbols used, and includes a mutual understanding of words in their meaning and also in their grammatical relationships. In familiar surroundings and in a familiar tongue, we ordinarily take this common information for granted and never consciously apply the rules that govern our expression. Most of us who studied English grammar thought it was a bore and tried to forget it as soon as we passed the course. Nevertheless, all our communication in English is based on this foundational content. But if we seriously study the English Bible with any confidence that God is speaking through it in verbally-inspired tones, we had better pay conscious attention to language in its detailed use of words, sentences, paragraphs, idioms, grammatical structure, and all. For those of you who feel the need of a quickie refresher course on English grammar, Appendix A in the back of the book will be of interest.

We need to remember that originally the Bible was not written in English but in Hebrew and Greek. What we are reading today are simply *translations* into English. In this connection, we must also recognize that each language has its peculiar word usage and grammar, and that a knowledge of these peculiarities will enhance our understanding of the text. We should also recognize that languages are living, growing things—constantly changing with changes in usage. Words start with a root meaning, are adapted to various derived meanings, and sometimes end up expressing the very opposite of their original content.

We can see that the Bible interpreter's task is complicated by these facts: (1) the Bible was recorded centuries ago in what are now ancient languages, (2) most of us don't read it in its original language, and (3) it was delivered to people with widely different cultural backgrounds from ours. Thus, we must be careful to hear the word in its cultural and temporal setting: yet its truth transcends all temporal, racial, language, and cultural boundaries.

Some Encouraging Words

In case you're getting discouraged, let me hasten to add that there is ample source material in English for you to delve into the Hebrew language without knowing Hebrew, and the Greek language without knowing Greek. How does that strike you? To me it adds an additional element of intrigue, and encourages me to be a good word detective. It's amazing what one can discover with a little bit of diligent research.

Which Version?

People often wonder which English translation of the Bible they should use, and they are troubled by the multiplicity of versions available today. I'd like to suggest that this is not a problem, but a blessing. Each translation represents untold hours of careful scholarship through which the translators endeavored to carry over the best sense of the original language. No translation is a perfect expression of the original, simply because there are often no word-for-word equivalents in the two languages. That's why biblical scholars study Hebrew and Greek, plus a number of related languages, to get as close as possible to the original *intent*. All of the scholarly translations, however, are sufficiently accurate to be trusted to give us an understanding of the truth. So, whether you choose to study the New American Standard Version, the Revised Standard Version, the New International Version, or the older King James Version, you can hear God speak to you through any of them.

The most practical way to resolve a problem in the English text is to compare translations when in doubt, even utilizing the paraphrases, such as *Phillips' New Testament* and *The Living Bible*. When using these, however, it is wise to rest your confidence more heavily on the standard versions. In my opinion, the Phillips translation has stayed much closer to the original language than *The Living Bible,* but either paraphrase is useful *if you are careful to compare and weigh the different renderings. Eternity* magazine published a helpful review of English versions which is listed in the bibliography in the Appendix.

3

The Goal of Bible Study

It is imperative to have some idea of the goal of our study of the Bible. Otherwise our motivation fades and we fail to be serious about our interpretive efforts. The most encouraging article I have ever read in this regard is the serious but keenly humorous piece written by Bernard Ramm.*

BUT IT ISN'T BIBLE STUDY

By Bernard Ramm

Scene I

I hurried to the morning hour hungry of soul. It would be the "Bible" hour. Amidst the high-pressure appeals of the conference for personal witnessing, world missions, and consecration, this would be one glad hour in which we would shut out the appeals of man and contemplate the inexhaustible word of God. The Scriptures were opened and read. My soul now drew near, eager for the exposition of the word of God. But down my open throat was stuffed another sermon! It was a good and proper sermon, but it wasn't Bible study. The speaker wheeled back and forth like an eagle over the text, but he never came to rest upon it. I left the hall as hungry as I came and quite sure that the speaker could not

---

* Printed in *Eternity* Magazine, February 1960 and used by permission of the publishers, the Evangelical Foundation Inc., Philadelphia, Pa.

distinguish between a sermon and a Bible study. *Sermonizing is not Bible study.*

Scene II

The honorable reverend stood before the audience and announced that he had the responsibility for the Bible study and would we all turn to a certain passage in the Old Testament. I thanked the Lord for a man who took his Bible study seriously, and eagerly anticipated a fruitful 45 minutes of real Bible exposition. After the text was read there issued a torrent of words exhorting us to five different things. God knows that we needed at least ten exhortations, but God also knows that the relationship of the text to the exhortations was completely accidental. Although I left the auditorium completely equipped with exhortations my added insight into the text was zero. *Whipping up three or four good exhortations from a text is not Bible study.*

Scene III

I crouched low in the pew. It was eventide Bible hour and I was praying for grace to endure another sermon or a fist full of miscellaneous exhortations falsely known as "Bible" study. The first paragraph of the speaker brought me snappily out of my crouch. I was not going to get various and divers exhortations but real, honest, undiluted Bible study! He opened the Bible and went after the text!

But at the third paragraph I was dismayed. From Bible study we slipped into exegesis. "The jussive means this" was followed by "the aorist participle means that." The housewives present did not know the difference between the jussive and lemon juice and their blank faces were rather faithful counterparts of their minds at this moment. For the first time in their lives the laymen heard the word "aorist" and surmised it was one of the pagan gods of the Hittites. Next we were hurriedly pulled past the opinions of Robertson, Denney, Cullmann and Broadus. By this time most of the little group was wool-gathering or day-dreaming or thinking how to damn with faint praise in the post-benediction chit-chat. *Academic exegesis is not Bible study.*

Scene IV

I mingled with a crowd of university students as we retreated from the hot sun into the cool auditorium. Certainly this crowd would put the speaker on the spot and force him to give out with good Bible study. The reputation of the Bible teacher preceded him like the runners preceded the ancient chariots. Away from the warm southern sun I sat smugly in my seat and said to myself, "This is it—real Bible study"!

The great Bible teacher strode across the platform like a great musician and putting his Bible upon the pulpit waited for the audience to quiet down before he played the first note. The con-

cert began. Like the fingers of the pianist race up and down the keyboard, so his fingers raced through the Bible finding the relevant verses. Plunk, ping, plunk! It did not take long before I realized that we were not having Bible study but a party line. The Bible was the keyboard and the teacher was playing his own tune upon it. The melody was not that of the Scripture but one imposed upon it by the Bible teacher. When the last embellishments were over, and when we were assured with a certainty the papacy could envy that we had the truth we were dismissed.

I did not feel blessed nor fed nor led deeper into the Scriptures. I felt brain-washed. I felt my share in the priesthood of the believers as it pertained to Bible study had been violated by the arrogant dogmatisms of a party line. *Propagandizing is not Bible study.*

Scene V

Every church has its Bible study time at the prayer service. Here there is no urgency to evangelize or exhort. The pastor may unhurriedly open the Sacred Text and feed the flock from its riches.

But as I watched the good man I almost cried. He announced his passage for the study and went to work—but what work! In his attempt to explain the text he was like a chicken with defective pecking aim. The poor hen pecks all around the corn but never hits it. She squints with her beady eye, she cocks her head, and then she pecks—and misses. She over-shoots or under-shoots.

So the poor man of God does everything but explain the text. I got 30 minutes of various and divers unrelated and uninspiring pious observations. Each observation was a worthy one. But the passage itself remained untouched. We had been all around the text but never in it. *Pious observations are not Bible study.*

The tragedy is that Bible study is so simple, yet so elusive. It is unfortunate that there is so much stamping around the scriptures with no real Bible study. Let me set down a few principles of what I believe constitutes real study of the Bible.

REAL BIBLE STUDY

First, *Bible study is in the language of the people, and in a fairly common translation.* Bible study intends to acquaint Christians with the contents of the Bible in their language, and in the Bible they read. An expert Bible teacher will know his Hebrew and Greek and will have consulted the authoritative works of reference. But when he stands before his class all this must be veiled or cloaked. The bones of basic research must not protrude. He must translate all his learning into the common language. Some reference to the original languages is not objectionable but the main burden of the study must rest upon the English language and a common translation.

If Bible study is to have staying power it must be in the common language and in a common text. The people will grasp the content of Scripture only as it is taught to them in the language in which they converse, pray, read and sing.

Exegesis is for the scholars and Bible study is no substitute for scholarly exegesis. But academic exegesis is not for the popular platform. Here God's people must be fed in their mother tongue.

Secondly, *the actual goal of Bible study is to convey the meaning to the people of a set number of verses.* Unless a manageable length is determined in advance the Bible study will be frustrating. Too much will have to be said in too short a time. Care must be taken to limit the scope of the study unless the teacher is giving some sort of general survey.

Next, the Bible teacher must attempt to convey the essential meaning of the text or passage. This is by far the most difficult task in Bible study—this *is* Bible study! Here is where the men are separated from the boys. Here is where fuzzy thinking is unfortunately put upon public display; or where real skill in handling the Word of God blesses the audience.

It is the presupposition of all interpretation of documents that the authors of these documents intended to set down a meaning in writing. *Therefore, if sufficient pains are taken, the meaning of the author may be recovered. All interpretation of documents—* be it a fragment of the pre-Socratic philosophers or a page from some medieval mystic—*has as its goal the recovery of the meaning of the author.*

Bible exegesis is the recovery of the meaning of the writers of Holy Writ; Bible study has the same goal only is less technical and less scholarly, and more popular and more devotional. *The heart of Bible Study must always be the matter of meaning.* The first question of Bible study is not: "What is devotional here?" nor "What is of practical importance here?" nor "What is inspirational here?" but *"What does this passage mean?"*

If the Bible teacher has no sensitivity to the question of meaning, there will be no real Bible study, but only a series of pious observations or a quiver full of exhortations or some interesting but pointless story-telling. *The one trait all great teachers of Scripture have had in common is their sensitivity to the meaning of the text.*

Sensitivity

This means sensitivity to *words*. The good interpreter never looks at a word without a question mark in his mind: He may consult his Greek lexicon, or his Webster's, or a commentary; or a concordance. But he fusses around among his books till the word upon which he has fixed his attention begins to glow with meaning.

An experienced doctor has a wonderful sensitivity in his fingers. He has spent a lifetime feeling lumps, swellings, growths, tumors, and wens. He knows their textures, their shapes and their peculiarities. Where our fingers tell us two things, a doctor's finger might tell him a dozen things. Just as a doctor's fingers have a feel for lumps and growths, so a Bible teacher must have feel for words. He must pass the fingers of his mind over their shapes, textures, and peculiarities.

This means sensitivity to *phrases, clauses, paragraphs,* and *idioms*. A good Bible teacher is restless; he takes nothing for granted. He is the detective whose victim is *the meaning* and the words in their various combinations of phrases, sentences, and paragraphs are the clues. Out of the various configurations of the words he delves for the meaning. He looks for the train of thought (i.e., the sequence *in meaning*) and tries to follow it throughout the passage. He works, digs, meditates, ruminates, and studies until the meaning of the text shines through.

It is right at this point where the poor teacher fails. He is content with his efforts even though his thoughts are vague, and his impressions are indistinct. As soon as he gets a good exhortation or practical application he is content and rests at that point. He does not sit with a restless mind and dig and sweat till he has achieved the meaning of the text. He does not reconstruct the brief of the Biblical text so that he can recite it to his audience. Failing to recover the essential meaning of the text, all he can do is offer a series of religious observations or a sermon in the place of a Bible study.

The good teacher, to the contrary, *keeps up a running flow of questions about meanings.* What does this word mean? What is the import of this phrase? Is this expression an idiom? What figure of speech is this? What is the connection of this verse with those before and after it? Who is this man? Where is this city? What Jewish custom is behind this practice? Where else in Scripture is this person or this theme treated? And certainly the good teacher will surround himself with those books which can answer these kind of questions.

Thirdly; Bible study always includes the relevant application of the text to the lives and times of the hearers. The Scriptures are the milk for babes in Christ, and strong food for the men in Christ. Bible study is feeding the people of God. But this feeding looks in two directions: (1) it looks to the truth of Scripture as it is in itself; and (2) it looks to the actual concrete situation of the listening audience. *The meaning of Scripture must be meaningfully applied to the lives of the Christians if Bible study is to be a meaningful activity.*

A good Bible teacher will make the proper doctrinal application. He may call attention to *the doctrinal importance* of a passage. If, for example, he is discussing II Corinthians 5 he can readily explain the great doctrines of reconciliation and atonement found in the chapter. Or, he may show how a cult or a sect abuses the doctrinal content of a passage; or he may indicate how the passage rebuts some view of a cult or sect.

A good Bible teacher explains the *correctives* for our spiritual life or Christian work found within the passage. If the selection is about prayer he will point out how our present practice of prayer needs the correction of this passage.

A good Bible teacher calls attention to the *comfort* and *encouragement* for God's people found in the text. It may be the invitation to prayer; or the certainty of the divine hearing. It may be the power of the intercessory work of Christ, or the enabling of the indwelling of the Holy Spirit, or the consolation of the providence of God.

Finally, a good Bible teacher calls attention to the *devotional* elements of the text. He shows wherein we should love God, or why we must follow Christ. He dwells upon the wonders of God's love, or Christ's death, or the Spirit's ministry to the saints. He attempts to excite our love and adoration, and seeks to lead us to . a deeper spirit of consecration.

I feel that I have experienced a good session of Bible study:
—when I felt that the teacher took me right into the text and not around it.
—when I felt we interacted with the text itself and not with the party-line beliefs of the teacher.
—when I felt that I had a better understanding of the text than when I came into the session.
—when I felt that the time was basically spent in meanings and not in a miscellany of religious platitudes.
—and when I have felt challenged, comforted, encouraged, and practically instructed.

This is such a good explanation of what really constitutes Bible study that I find myself rereading it periodically to renew my own approach to study and teaching.

Before we leave this consideration, I'd like to highlight two pertinent points:

(1) the good Bible student seeks to develop a *sensitivity to words,* including grammatical and idiomatic usage, and
(2) *he keeps up a running flow of questions about meanings.*

Whether we study for our own personal profit and growth or to teach the truth to others, the objective is the same—to get at the real meaning and significance of the text.

4

Interpretive Principles

So you have your Bible in hand. Now, what are the basic principles to observe as you begin to study it? Let me list some for you, then discuss each one. Please check out the references given for illustration on your own, as we seek to illustrate and apply these principles, will you?

Principles of Bible Interpretation

1. *Listen to Your Teacher!*
   Approach your study with a teachable, expectant attitude, desiring to be taught of God.

2. *Discover the Writer's Intent*
   Put yourself in the writer's sandals, and setting aside your preconceptions, aim to recover the writer's intent—including the intent of the ultimate Author, which sometimes goes beyond even the understanding of the human writer (e.g., 1 Peter 1:10–12 on the prophets).

3. *Interpret Literally*
   Accept the usual, literal sense of the words unless you have reason to believe they are figurative or allegorical. Interpret figurative language in the same way we use it in normal speech.

4. *Observe the Context*
Interpret in the light of the setting. Harmonize with the local and larger context, also the total context of biblical truth.

5. *Relate to the Historical/Cultural Setting*
Interpret with the historical and cultural setting in mind. It can make a great difference as to how we understand what is being said.

6. *Consider the Literary Mold*
The literary mold in which the language is cast is often crucial to our interpretation. Is it poetry? If so, that makes a difference, e.g., the Psalms.

7. *Observe the Author's Scope and Plan*
Every portion of the scripture does not cover every subject, so we must interpret in accord with the author's scope and plan, being consistent with the aim of God's total revelation.

8. *Compare Scripture with Scripture*
View corollary passages alongside the passage you are studying. Clear up problem areas with the clear teaching of other passages relating to the same subject.

9. *Study Word Meanings and Grammar*
Our normal tendency is to assume more than we really understand, thus arriving at a superficial view. We must observe word meanings and grammatical relationships *carefully*.

10. *Remember, God Speaks in Human Terms*
Recognize God's gracious accommodation of our limited, finite understanding by the use of human language in terms that men can grasp.

11. *Use the Original Languages*

In difficult interpretive problems, check the original language as the final authority. Many times (though not always), this will give the added light we need.

Now let's look at these interpretive principles in somewhat greater detail.

Basic Principles of Bible Interpretation

1. *Listen to Your Teacher!*

It always amazes me to recall that God himself wants to be our teacher. His word on the subject is this:

And as for you, the anointing which you received from Him abides in you, and *you have no need to have anyone teach you; but as His anointing teaches you about all things,* and is true and is not a lie, and just as it has taught you, you abide in Him (1 John 2:27 NASV, italics mine).

By this we understand that the Spirit of God, who lives in each believer, is our private tutor. Though God has given us pastors and teachers for our good (Eph. 4:11, 12), they are in addition to (and no substitute for) the Holy Spirit. This means that the humblest believer in Christ may be taught of God through his Word, even when human teachers are lacking.

The Lord Jesus makes it abundantly clear in these words,

When the Spirit of truth comes, *he will guide you into all the truth;* for he will not speak on his own authority, but whatever he hears he will speak, and he will declare to you the things that are to come. He will glorify me, for he will take what is mine and declare it to you (John 16:13, 14, italics mine).

Though the primary application of these words is to the eleven disciples whom he was addressing in this upper room scene, our Lord makes it clear that the Spirit's ministry of teaching would extend to all believers in Christ. For he says:

I do not pray for these only, but also for those who believe in me through their word (John 17:20).

2. *Discover the Writer's Intent*

Much Bible study is done to verify men's preconceptions, since all of us bring our personal opinions and biases with us. But honesty demands that we start with a clean page on which God may write his thoughts. If we can use our sanctified imagination to put ourselves in the writer's place and see things through his eyes, we will open up the windows of our minds to let in the light of God's truth. If God has really spoken through the pen of the human author, let's not try to rewrite the script. Proof-texting, i.e., quoting only those biblical texts which are useful to prove our own preconceived opinions and theological biases, is a favorite trick of the cultists and only succeeds in confusing the issue. We don't want to play that game. On the other hand, it is truly remarkable what we can discover when we *let God say what he has said.* We need to adopt this attitude:

> . . . and my speech and my message were not in plausible words of wisdom, but in demonstration of the Spirit and power, *that your faith might not rest in the wisdom of men but in the power of God* (1 Cor. 2:4, 5, italics mine).

> We have renounced disgraceful, underhanded ways; *we refuse to practice cunning or to tamper with God's word,* but by the open statement of the truth we would commend ourselves to every man's conscience in the sight of God (2 Cor. 4:2, italics mine).

3. *Interpret Literally*

We should view the Scripture just as we would any other writing, accepting the words at face value without the imposition of hidden meanings. This is the general rule, to which there are notable and recognizable exceptions, such as allegory and typology. Figures of speech are to be interpreted in the literal significance that the figure conveys. We will look at these special considerations in more detail in Chapters 7 through 9.

When the Scripture says, *"Rejoice always, pray constantly, give thanks in all circumstances; for this is the will of God in Christ Jesus for you"* (1 Thess. 5:16–18), we don't have a problem of interpreting the language, but rather one of how to *apply* the truth. We accept the literal meaning of the words. How we can *do* what it commands we must discover in the context: "Do not quench the Spirit," [for he is our strengthener to enable] "do not despise prophesying," [for preaching and teaching are the vehicle he uses to encourage us] *"but test everything;"* [for our thinking is askew and we are being fooled by an enemy if we are defeated on these issues] *"hold fast what is good,"* [for that is what will save the day] *"abstain from every form of evil"* (1 Thess. 5:19–22). Abstain, because indulging in evil gets us into trouble. The punch line is verse 24, *"He who calls you is faithful, and he will do it."* This assures us that the Lord is active in our behalf to enable us to do all he commands. So we take language in its literal sense when it is used like this.

But when we read, *"I am the vine, you are the branches"* (John 15:5), we recognize figurative language and seek the literal meaning of the figure. As we observe the context we read also, *"Abide in me, and I in you"* (John 15:4) and easily recognize that our Lord is talking about a *shared life,* since a branch is a living part of the vine, receiving the flow of life from it.

4. *Observe the Context*

The content immediately surrounding the text being studied always bears significant relationship to it which usually determines its meaning. This is by far the most important rule of Bible interpretation. Grammar and syntax are important, but in relative weight the context is the heavier import. Linguist

Anthony Burgess states humorously that studying grammar is "utter madness." It appears to be a science but doesn't behave like one, one reason being that grammarians tend to look at language the way it ought to be rather than the way it is. So we must always view a passage or verse (1) in its immediate setting; (2) in the larger context of the chapter or book in which it stands; and (3) in the light of the total context of biblical revelation. Remember that though we see it in its parts and divisions, God wrote *ONE Book,* not sixty-six. The unity and interweaving design of the Bible makes clear that it is one Book with sixty-six chapters.

For example, we have just considered part of John 15. To relate verses 4 and 5 to the local context, we need to recall that this is the upper room scene, in which Christ was instructing and encouraging his men in view of his departure, and laying the foundation for the yet-future beginning of the church. The theme in this chapter is fruit-bearing, i.e. how to have a fulfilled and productive life. His major thrust is the declaration, ". . . apart from me you can do nothing" (v. 5), and his aim is to get them (and us) to rest in his sufficiency, as a branch relates to the vine which sustains it.

Next, we set it in its place in John's Gospel, finding that the action is just before our Lord went to the cross. Then we recall that John's declared purpose for writing is ". . . *that we might have life in his name,"* that is, through the name of Jesus (John 20:31). So we have related our text to the Gospel of John.

We can go on from there to recognize that what Christ began he commissioned the apostles to complete, so we can relate what Christ said in the upper room to what the Apostle Paul wrote in his New Testament letters. I've tried to do this, and the result is in chart form for you to assess. You can undoubtedly add much to this chart; it is more suggestive than exhaustive. Here we have related to the larger biblical context and observed that it all fits together. God wrote *ONE Book,* using many penmen.

What CHRIST said . . . in the Upper Room	*SUBJECT*	*What PAUL said . . .* in his N.T. Letters.
JOHN 13—A SERVANT HEART: LOVE ONE ANOTHER "A new commandment . . . that you love . . . as I have loved you." v. 34	*BODY LIFE* Helping one another to keep in fellowship with Christ.	*"Have this mind . . .* which is yours in Christ Jesus, . . . who taking the form of *a servant . . .* obedient unto death . . . a cross." Phil. 2:5–8
JOHN 14—PERFECT PROVISION (a) *FOR THE FUTURE* "In my Father's house are many rooms . . ." v. 2 (b) *FOR THE PRESENT* "I will pray the Father . . . He will give you another counselor . . . the Spirit of truth . . ." vv. 16, 17	*REDEMPTION IN ETERNITY* "at home" with the Lord. *IN TIME* "at home" in the body. 2 Cor. 5:6–8	*"In (Christ) we have redemption* through his blood, the forgiveness of our trespasses, according to the riches of his grace . . ." Eph. 1:7 "It is no longer I who live, but *Christ* who *lives in me . . ."* Gal. 2:20 ". . . shall we be *saved by his life"* Rom. 5:10
*JOHN 15—ADEQUATE RESOURCES A SHARED LIFE—*Vine and branches. "He who abides in me, and I in him . . . bears much fruit, for apart from me you can do nothing." v. 5	*NEW COVENANT* USEFULNESS DEPENDENCE	*"We have this treasure in earthen vessels,* to show that the transcendent power belongs to God and not to us." 2 Cor. 4:7 ". . . our competence is from God, who has made us competent . . ." 2 Cor. 3:5, 6
JOHN 16—OVERCOMING OPPOSITION ". . . whoever kills you will think he is offering service *to God."* v. 2 ". . . the Counselor . . . *will convince the world* (1) *Concerning sin* (missing out on life, no reality, no fulfillment) (2) *Righteousness* (value systems wrong, so no sense of worth), and (3) *Judgment . . .* (don't know Satan's hold has been broken, so no freedom) v. 7–11	*SPIRITUAL WARFARE* ACTIVE HATRED CHRIST HAS DEFEATED SATAN *LOVE WINS*	*"Put on the whole armor of God,* that you may be able to stand fast against the wiles of the devil. For we are not contending against flesh and blood, but against . . . the spiritual hosts of wickedness . . ." Eph. 6:11–13 "*(Christ) disarmed the principalities and powers,* and made a public example of them, *triumphing over them in the cross."* Col. 2:15 Therefore, ". . . if your enemy is hungry, feed him . . ." Rom. 12:20
JOHN 17—A PERFECT PRAYER (1) "Holy Father, *keep them . . ."* v. 11 (2) *"Sanctify them* in the truth . . ." v. 17 (3) "As thou didst send me into the world, so *I have sent them* into the world." v. 18 (4) *"That they all may be one . . . so that the world may believe* thou hast sent me." v. 21 (5) "I am praying . . . *for those whom thou hast given me . . ."* v. 9	*SECURITY CONFIDENCE* *PURPOSE* *UNITY* the basis of evangelism *GOD'S GIFT to HIS SON . . . YOU!*	". . . you . . . were sealed with the promised Holy Spirit . . . the guarantee of our inheritance . . ." Eph. 1:13,14 ". . . he who began a good work in you will bring it to completion . . ." Phil. 1:6 "So we are ambassadors for *Christ, GOD* making his appeal through us." 2 Cor. 5:20 "There is one body and one Spirit . . . one Lord, one faith, one baptism, one God and Father . . ." Eph. 4:4–6 Praying . . . "that you may know . . . what are the riches *of his glorious inheritance in the saints . . ."* Eph. 1:18

5. *Relate to the Historical and Cultural Setting*

We are prone to interpret everything we read in terms of our twentieth century Western culture, since that's the sphere in which we live. It takes a conscious effort to research and absorb some of the data that will make our thoughts conform to the time and culture of the writer. Much of this can be accomplished through the use of Bible Dictionaries, and books on the history and archeology of Old and New Testament times. Edersheim's *Life and Times of Jesus, the Messiah* is a classic work on the cultural features of biblical times. Old and New Testament introductions also help us get the feel and flavor of life in Bible times. The bibliography in the Appendix will give you further source materials on this subject.

To illustrate the principle we have before us: it is helpful, when studying the Book of Hebrews, to remember that it was written while the temple was still standing in Jerusalem. This makes clear the need for the strong appeal to these early Hebrew Christians to "go forth to him [Jesus] outside the camp, bearing abuse for him. For here we have no lasting city, but we seek the city which is to come" (Heb. 13:13, 14). And, "We have an altar from which those who serve the tent have no right to eat" (Heb. 13:10). There was strong temptation for these early Christians to be drawn back into the "shadows" of the temple worship forms and away from the reality of Christian faith.

Observing this, we can better understand the strong warnings in the book. After all, it was written *to the Hebrews* of the first century. Our interpretation should be based on this historical/cultural setting, with application to our contemporary Western scene flowing out of that interpretation. It then becomes obvious that there are many similar situations where modern men and women halt short of true faith, settling for religious ritual instead. The same strong warnings can then be applied properly to present situations. The following outline illustrates how applicable this truth is, almost twenty centuries after its writing.

DON'T MISS MELCHIZEDEK!

We need to advance from the Aaronic priesthood (the Law) to the Melchizedek priesthood, which portrays the adequacy and resources of Christ as our risen, living Lord. In view of Christ's availability to us as our great High Priest after the order of Melchizedek, to strengthen us for every test and supply our every need, consider these warnings from Hebrews:

1. THE DANGER OF DRIFTING   Hebrews 2:1–3
   The Problem: Inattention
   The possibility of drifting.
   The Test: Are You Listening?

2. THE DANGER OF AN UNBELIEVING   Hebrews 3:12–19
   HEART
   The Problem: Hearing, but not *Believing*
   The possibility: hardening of the heart.
   The Test: How Well Do You Rest?

3. THE DANGER OF PROLONGED IMMA-   Hebrews 6:1–8
   TURITY
   The Problem: Being Long-Time Babies
   The possibility: missing the value of
   the Melchizedek priesthood.
   The Test: Are You Really Going Anywhere?

4. THE DANGER OF MISSING REALITY—see-   Hebrews 10:26–31
   ing just the shadow.
   *The Problem: Failing to Respond to
   Grace*
   The possibility of spurning the Son.
   *The Test: How Real Is Jesus Christ to
   You?*

5. THE DANGER OF CONTRADICTION   Hebrews 12:15–29
   *The Problem: The Practical Denial of
   Christ's Lordship*
   The possibility of refusing him the
   right to give orders.
   *The Test: How Well Do You Worship
   through Obedience to Christ?*

"Through him then let us continually offer up a sacrifice of praise to God, that is, the fruit of lips that acknowledge his name. Do not neglect to do good and to share what you have, for such sacrifices are pleasing to God" (Heb. 13:15, 16).

"Now may the God of peace who brought again from the dead our Lord Jesus, the great shepherd of the sheep, by the blood of the *eternal covenant,* equip you with everything good that you may do his will, *working in you* that which is pleasing in his sight, *through Jesus Christ;* to whom be glory for ever and ever. Amen" (Heb. 13:20, 21).

6. *Consider the Literary Mold*

The Bible is history, prophecy, prose narrative, poetry, discourse, persuasive argumentation, exhortation, instruction, illustration, and more. It includes the use of parables, proverbs, fables, riddles, enigmas, symbols, and various kinds of analogies—virtually every kind of figurative use of language. Sound interpretive study will view each scripture in the mold in which it is cast.

Poetic language is obviously more colorfully figurative than prose language forms. When the psalmist says,

Bless the Lord, O my soul!
O Lord my God, thou art very great!
Thou art clothed with honor and
majesty
who coverest thyself with light as
with a garment,
who hast stretched out the heavens
like a tent,
who hast laid the beams of thy chambers
on the waters,
who makest the clouds thy chariot,
who ridest on the wings of the wind,
who makest the winds thy messengers,
fire and flame thy ministers (Ps. 104:1–4).

we easily recognize poetic expression designed to give us a sense of the greatness and majesty of God in his creative supremacy over the natural world.

On the other hand, when we read:

Follow the pattern of sound words which you have heard from me, in the faith and love which are in Christ Jesus; guard the truth that has been entrusted to you by the Holy Spirit who dwells within us (2 Tim. 1:13, 14).

we see that it is not poetry, but a strong charge from Paul to Timothy, being commanded with all the weight of Paul's apostolic authority.

Again, we easily recognize the story-form narrative style of the Gospels and receive them as eyewitness accounts.

7. *Observe the Author's Scope and Plan*

Every book of the Bible does not treat every subject. On the contrary, each book covers a limited scope of subject matter which is not always announced by the writer, but is always discernible if we observe carefully.

The plan of a book is that orderly progression of thought the writer had in mind when he wrote.

A panoramic view of the book as a whole is needed to ascertain these features. This means reading and re-reading until our observation and analysis uncover the writer's intent and trace his thought pattern. At first glance, some books of the Bible seem to have no progression or order, but I have discovered that deeper study invariably reveals the outline. Quite often the problem is ours, not the writer's, in that we have gained only a superficial view of the scope and plan imbedded in the text. There is no substitute for careful, diligent study to gain this information. And when we finally see it, it often forms the outline that frames the book in our minds and begins to make it ours.

For instance, the scope of John's Gospel is clearly the presenting of Jesus Christ as the Messiah, the Son of God. His aim in this testimony is to lead his hearers to faith in Christ, that they might have the eternal life he offers. We see this stated in:

. . . these are written that you may believe that Jesus is the Christ, the Son of God, and that believing you may have life in his name (John 20:31).

By reading the book this statement is confirmed.

John's first epistle has quite another aim. It is written that we might enjoy the reality of fellowship with Christ and the assurance that brings to our hearts. We see this in 1 John 1:3 and 4,

> that which we have seen and heard we proclaim also to you, so that you may have fellowship with us; and our fellowship is with the Father and with his Son Jesus Christ. And we are writing this that our joy may be complete.

and

> I write this to you who believe in the name of the Son of God, that you may know that you have eternal life (1 John 5:13).

Paul's letter to the Romans is aimed at the logical exposition of the gospel of God (Rom. 1:1–5), and his plan is to show that the whole world (pagan, moralist, and religionist) stands guilty before God (Rom. 3:10–20), so that any who come by faith in the One who died for us and rose again might be justified by faith, apart from works.

> For no human being will be justified in his sight by works of the law, since through the law comes knowledge of sin. But now the righteousness of God has been manifested apart from law, although the law and the prophets bear witness to it, the righteousness of God through faith in Jesus Christ for all who believe. For there is no distinction; since all have sinned and fall short of the glory of God, they are justified by his grace as a gift, through the redemption which is in Christ Jesus, whom God put forward as an expiation by his blood, to be received by faith (Rom. 3:20–25).

> . . . Jesus our Lord . . . was put to death for our trespasses and raised for our justification (Rom. 4:24, 25).

The plan of the Book of Romans then includes how the gospel works out in life (chapter 5–8); explains how Israel fits into

God's purposes in the gospel (chapters 9–11); appeals for a life style consistent with the character of the One who redeemed us (chapters 12–15); and concludes with personal greetings to some who have responded to the gospel (chapter 16), with a final benediction focused around the new information the gospel reveals and its importance to all men (Rom. 16:25–27).

The scope of Peter's letters (1 and 2 Peter) is the problem of suffering Christians, and his plan is to unfold to us how we can cope with all that life throws at us.

We often outline a book to show its plan. Several examples of this are included in Chapter 12, and in the Appendix.

8. *Compare Scripture with Scripture*

There are many complementary passages in the Bible which shed light on each other. The interpreter must read them all to gain the composite picture. The Old Testament is frequently quoted in the New Testament, and we seriously err if we do not read the whole content of the passage being quoted. We must remember that most of the New Testament writers were Jews who knew their Old Testament scriptures as you and I probably never will. Their minds gathered the quoted material from memory, whereas you and I don't have it stored away to recall. So we must read the full account from the record.

9. *Check the Old Testament Reference*

To illustrate the Old Testament quotations in the New Testament: for years I had read 1 Corinthians 14 without noticing the Old Testament quotation in verse 21. Here the apostle quoted Isaiah 28:11 with reference to speaking in tongues.

. . . By men of *strange tongues* and by the lips of foreigners will I speak to *this people,* and even then they will not listen to me, says the Lord (1 Cor. 14:21, italics mine).

As I finally took the time to read the Old Testament reference which I found in the margin of my Bible, I discovered some remarkable facts: (1) Isaiah 28 is a picture of the terrible judgment of God on his disobedient people; (2) intermingled in the judgment scene are references to the gracious ministry of God through his Son, like:

> In that day the Lord of hosts will be a crown of glory, and a diadem of beauty, to the remnant of his people (Isa. 28:5).

Also,

> Behold I am laying in Zion for a foundation a stone, a tested stone, a precious cornerstone, of a sure foundation: "he who believes will not be in haste" (Isa. 28:16).

Note "the remnant" in verse 5 and the obvious reference to the Lord Jesus in verse 16, as confirmed by Peter in 1 Peter 2:6–8. So, in Isaiah 28, we have *mercy* in the midst of *judgment*.

Then, notice that according to 1 Corinthians 14:21, God is speaking through the strange tongues to "this people," which clearly refers to Israel. I see here the purpose for which God has given the gift of tongues—to be a "sign" (verse 22) to those first century Jews, a sign that God was acting in judgment against their stubborn unbelief, with mercy available to them in the midst of his wrath.

It becomes most significant, then, that "tongues" on the day of Pentecost (as recorded in Acts 2), have a distinct and unique purpose: to alert the Jews that their day of privilege was over, and that God was now welcoming Jew and Gentile alike by faith in the Lamb of God who takes away sin and saves sinners, whether Jewish sinners or Gentile sinners, on the ground of his death and resurrection. Thus, "tongues" marked the end of God's dealing with the world through the nation Israel, and the beginning of the new era of the church. Much more could be said to pursue this clue from the Old Testament, but perhaps this is enough to illustrate the point.

Topical Bible Study

An expansion of this principle is topical Bible study. Since the total content of the biblical revelation on any one topic is scattered through the Bible, we must gather all the information to get the total comprehensive view. Topical Bibles like Nave's, or Thompson's Chain Reference Bible, or the connected references in the Scofield Bible and its subject index, help us in this kind of study. Tracing through the total biblical information from Genesis to Revelation on a particular subject is a rewarding experience. For instance, one can start at Genesis 3 in a topical or chain-reference Bible and trace the total teaching of the Scriptures on Satan clear through to Revelation 20:10 where we see the end of his nefarious career. We need to keep in mind when we do this, however, that the information is not necessarily chronological as it is placed in the text.

Comparing parallel passages is another helpful way to gain interpretive insight. It makes sense to read accounts of the same events recorded in all the gospels, as one account will give information not recorded in the other, and thus give a much clearer picture of the content of both. There are harmonies of the Gospels that can help us to fit things together from the gospel records (see the Bibliography for these.)

10. *Remember, God Speaks in Human Terms*

Many interpretive problems can be avoided if we remember that God has scaled down his communication of truth to man's level. The Bible is anthropomorphic, i.e., God's eternal truth is brought down to human level and expressed in human terms.

Did I say I dislike big words? Well, I do, unless they are given meaning. This one, anthropomorphic, is a very descriptive term that says a lot if we simply define it. It's derived from two Greek words: *anthropos,* man, and *morphe,* form. It means "ascribing human form or attributes to beings or things not human, especially to a deity." In this mode of expression, God has stepped down into our shoes so that he can speak to us on our level of understanding.

So when we read "God repented" in Exodus 32:14, we understand that he is speaking in man's terms, and *from our viewpoint* he seems to have changed his mind. But if we review the character of God as revealed in the Scriptures, we find that he knows everything before it happens and never has to change his mind. He has all the information on any subject and never needs to second-guess himself like we do.

And when we read "God came down" as Exodus 3:8, we recognize this as the language of appearances. Since he is omnipresent, he was always there, but he uses this expression to convey the idea that now he is giving his full attention to the matter in question. These are anthropomorphisms.

11. *Use the Original Languages*

Many interpretive difficulties will be readily resolved by investigating the words behind the English text. For the unskilled in biblical Greek or Hebrew, it is still possible to get behind the English text to the original language through the

use of available exegetical tools in English. (And, just so I don't fog the atmosphere with meaningless words—exegetical means "to raise up out of," i.e., to expose the meaning.) It is truly remarkable how much has been done in English to furnish us with good exegetical tools.

Grappling with Greek

Vine's Expository Dictionary of New Testament Words is a veritable gold mine of information about New Testament Greek, which one can use without knowing a word of Greek. Every serious student of the Bible should have this volume. To illustrate its value, when we encounter the word *mystery* in the New Testament we can discover from Vine, among other things, this fact:

> Mystery—a spiritual truth revealed in the Gospel. In the ordinary sense a mystery implies *knowledge withheld;* its scriptural significance is *truth revealed.* In the New Testament it denotes . . . that which, being outside the range of unassisted natural apprehension, can be made known in a manner and at a time appointed by God, and to those only who are illumined by His Spirit.[1]

Two things one must realize about this book: (1) It is compiled from the vocabulary of the King James Version, so one must have that text from which to work; and (2) every time the author inserts a paragraph mark (¶) at the end of an entry it means he has cited every occurrence of the Greek word in the New Testament. This is a tremendous help, as it gives us a ready reference on one page which saves us much time and effort checking through the concordance.

Hebrew Word Study

The rough equivalent of this book for the Old Testament is Pick, *Dictionary of the Old Testament Words for English*

---

[1] W. E. Vine, *Vine's Expository Dictionary of New Testament Words* (Old Tappan, N.J.: Fleming H. Revell Co., n.d.), p. 97 (under M).

Readers. We can use this book, or we can turn to *Strong's Exhaustive Concordance* for information on the Hebrew of the Old Testament. We can learn a great deal from Hebrew words without being able to read Hebrew. For instance, Hebrew names have meanings that often shed light on Old Testament passages.

In the well-known story in Daniel 3, the three Hebrew children are called Shadrach, Meshach, and Abednego, which are Chaldean names given them by the king's eunuch (Dan. 1:7). But we read there that their Hebrew names were Hananiah, Mishael, and Azariah. Checking *Strong's Concordance,* we find in the Hebrew and Chaldee Dictionary portion (in the back) that Shadrach, Meshach, and Abednego are Chaldean names whose significance the concordance does not reveal, though other sources relate them to Babylonian deities, while:

> Hananiah means *the Lord has favored.* (see #2608, Strong's Concordance Hebrew entry) Mishael means *who is what God is?* (see entry #4332) and Azariah means *the Lord has helped.* (see entry #5838) The *iah* on the end of these names is the root of Jehovah, or Yahweh, the Lord God, and the suffix *el* on Mishael is the Hebrew word for the Almighty, referring to God.

As we read their story in Daniel 3, their names shine with meaning relating to the narrative: Hananiah knows the God of all grace, *the Lord who has favored,* while Mishael asks *"who is like the Almighty who is my God?",* and Azariah surely knows *Jehovah has helped,* even in a red-hot furnace— or, perhaps we should say, especially there.

Unger's Bible Dictionary is also a useful source of this kind of information.

□ 5 □

The Interpretive Process

Four major steps are involved in the interpretive process.
1. Careful Observation
2. Asking Interpretive Questions
3. Thinking through to an Interpretive Conclusion
4. Anchoring Our Interpretation in the Application of Interpretive Principles

Let's look at each of these in more detail.

1. *Careful Observation*

Here's where most of us either win or lose. Weak and inaccurate interpretation inevitably results from superficial or careless observation. Ours is the "instant" age, especially in America. We want "instant" everything it seems. But there is no such thing as instant understanding when we seek to interpret the Scriptures. We need to emulate some of the meticulous scholarship of the previous century. One wonders how a single lifetime would be long enough to produce some of the mammoth biblical scholarship of the past. I believe that if we applied ourselves as the earlier scholars did, we would discover depths of truth even they did not see, for we have the benefit of all the previous generations of scholarship. So, let's be good observers. First, we must immerse ourselves in the book we are studying by repeated readings of the whole book. There is no substitute for this. We need to treat it as if it were a love letter from the one who loves us the most.

Then we should change our approach to that of a news reporter, who must constantly ask and answer the *who, what, when, where, why,* and *how* of his subject.

Who is writing? About *whom?* And to *whom?*

About *what* is he writing? That is, we must try to discover the major subject he seeks to cover. *What* is the situation of writer and reader? *What* circumstances surround them? *What* is their nationality and cultural setting? *What* is their recent history? *What* is the exact meaning of the words used?

What literary form has the writer used: poetry, parable, narrative, history, logical argumentative discourse, prophecy?

When is the action taking place, especially in relation to the rest of biblical history?

Where is the action taking place? *Where* is the writer going with his argument? *Where* does he expect to carry his hearers?

Why is the book or passage being written? *Why* does the writer move from one topic to another in his discourse? *Why* is he angry, or excited, or pleading, or commanding, or exhorting?

How does he proceed to present his subject, through what logical steps or progress of thought? *How* does he seek to persuade his hearers? *How* does he relate personally to the message he is declaring? *How* does he introduce his subject? *How* does he conclude his communication? *How* is he motivated to write? *How* is he related to the ultimate Author of his book? *How* has he responded to the truth he is declaring? *How* have the intervening centuries clouded his content through changes in word meanings, cultural differences, and the changed viewpoints of modern man? *How* has he managed to communicate unchanging truth, in spite of all? *How* does his writing affect my approach to the facts of life and alter my life style?

You can see, we must really do our homework. Let me testify, however, that the result is worth it—for ourselves, and for those with whom we share God's truth.

Observing Word Meanings

Part of our observation is arriving at the clear meaning of words. To me, one of the most fascinating areas of study is investigating the exact, definitive content of individual words. After all, if we really don't understand the words in a sentence or paragraph, we can hardly expect to understand the thought or idea being communicated. And remember, our aim, as good Bible interpreters, is to get at the intended meaning of the writer. Apart from that, we are just playing games, probably to justify our preconceptions.

There are several veins we can mine in our digging for the hidden treasures of the word. Here are two of them.

⊤ Using the English dictionary

⊤ Exploring the meanings of Greek and Hebrew words used in the original language text.

For now, we'll stick with the English dictionary, leaving Hebrew and Greek for later chapters. The dictionary is perhaps one of the most valuable, and the most neglected, of the tools we can use to understand the English Bible. Think a minute; when was the last time you reached for the dictionary? I believe that most Christians would flunk a vocabulary test on some of the most basic and essential words used in the Bible. Try some of these: salvation, redemption, hope, faith, reconciliation, love, joy, peace, apostle, disciple, worship, fellowship, resurrection, life, death, holiness.

I hope you are *now* curious enough to check out some of these in your dictionary. Then go to a book like Vine's *Expository Dictionary of New Testament Words* and see what more is added to your understanding. Then write out your own definitions of these words, reflecting your own grasp of their import. Though it may sound boring, this can be a most ex-citing and enlightening exercise, one which can become a life-time habit of being a good word detective.

Then there's grammar—important, but neglected. Perhaps you need a quick refresher on basic grammatical data. See Appendix A.

2. & 3. *Asking Interpretive Questions and Thinking Through to Conclusions*

It seems that some of us read the Bible without ever asking ourselves a question. Whether we think it is unspiritual to do so, or whether we have been brainwashed by biblical dogma-tism, or whether we are just lazy-minded, the net result is the same. With this unthinking approach we will never become good Bible interpreters. I believe the Lord likes to have us ask questions, for this gives him the opportunity to give us answers. I honestly believe we cannot read the Scriptures intelligently without having a flood of questions.

Let's Try It!

For example, our Lord Jesus said to his men in the upper room:

Truly, truly, I say to you, he who believes in me will also do the works that I do, and greater works than these will he do, be-cause I go to the Father (John 14:12).

Here's one for us to interpret. For what he says seems so contrary to our experience, we hardly know whether to take him seriously, at first. But if we start to ask questions, hope-fully the light will begin to dawn. Here are some questions that come to mind. They are in italics so that you can follow my thinking.

First I note that our Lord's words tell me he is intensely serious: "Truly, truly, I say to you. . . ." This is a literary device like, "Now hear this! Now hear this!" He's trying to get our attention. So I begin seriously to confront the issues. My mind says, *What does he mean by "he who believes in me"? Does this refer to our initial faith which made us Christians, or does it refer to an ongoing faith?* I observe that he is trying to encourage his men in the life they face after he leaves, so I take it to be an emphasis on the latter, that is, "he who believes" is the one who, at each occasion, keeps on trusting him for enabling power and thus will be enabled to do the same things he has done. *And what had he done?* He had made lame men walk, blind men see. He even raised some from the dead! *And were these early disciples to be able to do that?* Well, the record of the Acts of the Apostles declares that they did.

But then I ask, *Why did our Lord do these things?* And it becomes clear, as I review the record, that he invariably had a deeper intent than physical healing. His greater concern was for the redemption and healing of the human soul and spirit. If this were not so, I think he would have set up a Jerusalem Healing Clinic, and everyone would have been healed. His aim was deeper than physical healing. He asked such questions as, "Which is easier, to say, 'Your sins are forgiven you,' or to say, 'Rise and walk'?" (Luke 5:23). He thereby sought to shift his hearers' thinking from the physical to the spiritual level.

So I conclude his meaning in the text we are interpreting is that they would not just be able to do what he had done, but that their doing so would be for the same purpose, and fulfilling the same plan, as he had in mind. As I view his miracles, I see that he did all under the direction of his Father, and only as required to fulfill his plan. I learn this from the immediate context, "Do you not believe that I am in the Father and the Father in me? The words that I say to you I do not speak on my own authority; but the Father who dwells in me does his works." And the broader context of John's Gospel (see John 5:19, 6:57, 8:38, & 12:49, 50).

What, then, is the purpose of his miracles? I see the answer in Luke 4:17–21 (italics mine):

> . . . and there was given to him the book of the prophet Isaiah. He opened the book and found the place where it was written, *"The Spirit of the Lord is upon me, because he has anointed me to preach good news to the poor. He has sent me to proclaim release to the captives and recovering of sight to the blind, to set at liberty those who are oppressed, to proclaim the acceptable year of the Lord."* And he closed the book, and gave it back to the attendant, and sat down; and the eyes of all in the synagogue were fixed on him. And he began to say to them, "Today this scripture has been fulfilled in your hearing."

in accord with our Lord's answer to John the Baptist in Matthew:

> Now when John heard in prison about the deeds of the Christ, he sent word by his disciples, and said to him, *"Are you he who is to come, or shall we look for another?"* And Jesus answered them, *"Go and tell John what you hear and see: the blind receive their sight and the lame walk, lepers are cleansed and the deaf hear, and the dead are raised up, and the poor have good news preached to them.* And blessed is he who takes no offense at me" (Matt. 11:2–6, italics mine).

Our Lord was (in Luke 4) presenting the credentials of his Messiahship, and John the Baptist was given those credentials in Matthew 11. Here we have moved to the larger context of the New Testament and even further, to the whole Bible, in the quotation Luke makes from Isaiah 61:1, 2. As a result, we see that the miracles of Jesus were the documentation of his Messiahship, to authenticate that he was truly the Christ, sent from God. We further conclude that the miracles of the apostles were a similar authentication of their being "sent ones" from God, which is the meaning of the word *apostle*.

Going to the next phrase of John 14:12, we face the really tough part: ". . . and greater works will he do . . ." The obvious question that comes to mind is, *What are the greater works? And how are they greater—in number or degree?* To answer this we further observe that he gives a reason for this statement of fact: ". . . because I go to the Father." So the next question is, *What difference will his going to the Father make?* Then we recall that his departure meant his going to the cross, his coming back in resurrection life, his sending of the Holy Spirit to indwell and empower the church, and his ascension to the right hand of the Father to intercede for his own. His disciples thought they were *losing* when he went away; he said they were *gaining*—that it was advantageous to them for him to go. From our vantage point in history, we can no doubt see this better than they did at the time he spoke these words.

So where are we now? *What are the greater works? Are they greater in degree or in number?* To answer the latter, I would suggest they are greater in *both* degree and number. *What is greater than the physical miracles?* Certainly the miracles of spiritual healing made possible by the cross, resurrection, and intercession of Christ. The Lord sought to make plain throughout his earthly life and ministry that the soul and spirit of man are far more important than the body, though he does not disdain the human body. And when one reviews the history of the Christian church, starting at Pentecost when some three thousand were saved and thinking through to the penetration of the gospel worldwide (including the fact that from eleven men it reached *us* nineteen centuries later and half a world away) it's not hard to see the greater works he envisioned, greater both in number and in degree, bringing eternal salvation. Nothing like what we can review in the history of the church ever occurred in our Lord's earthly ministry. And all this, "because I go to the Father," he said.

I think we have arrived at a fair understanding of what Jesus had in mind for his men in the upper room, but how does it apply to us today? Well, first we should observe that in John 17, our Lord prayed *for his own* who were with him then, but he also extended his prayer *to include all of us who are his* (see John 17:20). And if we take careful note, we see that in this upper room ministry, our Lord was laying the foundation of the church, instructing his men so they might understand what was happening when they came to the day of Pentecost, when the Spirit of God joined together the first members of the body of Christ to form the church. So, by extension and application, I believe the Lord would have us understand that believers in our day are empowered to do anything and everything he has in mind to further his redemptive purposes in the world—but only under his direction, enabled by his power, and consistent with his character and purpose. Finally, note that the next subject he introduces (in John 14:13, 14) is *prayer*—the expression of our utter dependence on him to do what he says he will do.

So we've tackled a rather difficult verse of scripture, asked our interpretive questions, and reached some conclusions as to its meaning. If you feel as I do about it, it is humbling, challenging, and exciting—even in the process—but well worth the effort. Look at the open door of ministry this verse represents in its total import, if we believe it. What a charter for encouraging and motivating us to action in cooperation with our Lord!

4. *Anchoring Our Interpretation in the Application of Interpretive Principles*

In summary, note how we employed some of the principles of Bible interpretation in the course of our study. We applied particularly the rule of context, observing the local, larger, and total biblical relationships. Though we could have gone further in this, we gained enough to answer our interpretive questions with some degree of understanding. We inquired into the purpose of miracles, looked at the Messiahship credentials of the Lord Jesus, and entered into the purposes of God in the church.

We did not apply *all* the interpretive principles we have

listed, but we used the ones that were necessary to arrive at a satisfactory conclusion. That's all we ever need to do, for our aim is to recover the meaning of the author or speaker, not just to get exercise in the use of rules.

We could go much further into this particular study, and I have done so on my own; but what I have described here is, I trust, sufficient to illustrate the process without wearing out your patience.

In all of this investigative action, we need to remember that:

⊤ The Bible is meant to be understood, for these are things God has revealed to us that we might know the things he has freely given to us.

⊤ It contains much that is easy to understand.

⊤ It has depths of meaning and portions that are hard to fathom.

⊤ It leaves some questions unanswered.

⊤ But we can gain from it all we really need to know to live fulfilled lives in right relation to God and to man.

My friend and fellow pastor, David Roper, is a master at asking interpretive questions. See the Appendix for his questions on 2 Timothy 1 and 2.

□ 6 □

Bible Study Approaches

Bible study begins in an attitude of prayer, whether expressed in words or quietly reflected in the heart. The expression of the psalmist is exactly what our hearts should say:

Open my eyes, that I may behold
    wondrous things out of thy law (Ps. 119:18).

Or, as the apostle prays for the Ephesian Christians,

. . . that the God of our Lord Jesus Christ, the Father of glory, may give you a spirit of wisdom and revelation in the knowledge of him, having the eyes of your hearts enlightened, that you may know . . . (Eph. 1:17, 18).

And the result should be:

My meditation of him shall be sweet: I will be glad in the Lord (Ps. 104:34 KJV).

We really are wholly dependent on God for the illumination of his Word to our minds and hearts. Methodology and techniques, though necessary, are fruitless unless we are truly taught of God.

With that desire, then, we can listen, search, compare, meditate, reach conclusions, and be ready to obey the truth we have discovered. When we have done this, we can expect God to give opportunity to share what we have learned with others, for he doesn't want us to keep a good thing to ourselves. Approaching our study with this attitude we can then use various means to enhance our understanding of the Bible.

There is one basic method of Bible study, but several different *approaches* utilizing that method. The method is the well-known OBSERVE, INTERPRET, and APPLY so well taught in Oletta Wald's *Joy of Discovery,* which is heartily recommended for your study (see bibliography in the appendix for details). It goes like this:

Observation—what it says

Interpretation—what it means

Application—what it means to me personally, that is, what
I must do about it

Three different approaches to Bible study are the *panoramic,* the *telescopic,* and the *microscopic.*

⊤ The *panoramic view* seeks to encompass the overall sweep and scope of the Bible or a passage of scripture. It's as if one were scanning the whole landscape from one horizon to the other from a high vantage point. If you have ever stood on a site near Glacier Point in Yosemite National Park where the whole sweep of mountains, valleys, rivers, and falls is stretched out before you as though on a gigantic canvas, you have a mental picture of this approach to Bible study. It has unique value to give us the sense of the Bible's cohesive unity through a wide variety of expression, observable only through the panoramic look at scripture.

⊤ The *telescopic view* is quite different. As a telescope limits the field of vision and focuses attention on one place at a time, so we can view the Bible. This is pictorial of topical study, with its focus upon a specific truth, theme, or word. In this approach we scan across the panorama of God's Word, focusing our attention on a particular area of truth, and then relate it to the whole picture.

⊤ The *microscopic view* is still another approach. Just as a microscope brings into view things ordinarily hidden to the human eye, so the carefully analytical and detailed study of the Bible reveals the hidden treasures of God's Word. And just as discovering hidden treasure brings excitement and delight, so it is when we examine the Bible this way. This type of study involves vocabulary and language study, includes the investigation of biblical history and culture, and demands an intensive, methodical approach to scripture. The results are eminently worthwhile, for we find God revealing to us the underlying pattern and purpose of his Word through our diligent use of this approach. Casual curiosity will never discover this hidden wealth.

Follow with me as we work through an illustration of each of these three modes of study, will you?

The Panoramic View

If we were to read the whole Bible, seeking to discover its central theme, we would see something like this:

The First Look—The Old Testament

The Old Testament, we can easily see, is centered around the Hebrew people, for as early as the eleventh chapter of Genesis, the book of beginnings, we are introduced to Abram, the first Hebrew, and the father of the nation Israel. God chose to work through this people and to make their history a living illustration of his own desire to relate to all of us on a basis of loving reality. The New Testament confirms this idea with these words, referring to Israel:

> Now *these things happened to them as an example, and they were written for our instruction,* upon whom the ends of the ages have come (1 Cor. 10:11 NASV, italics mine).

And

> . . . *whatever was written in earlier times was written for our instruction,* that through perseverance and the encouragement of

the Scriptures we might have hope (Rom. 15:4 NASV, italics mine).

So we see the Old Testament, with all its varied forms of expression, as essentially God's picture book, showing through the nation Israel God's yearning heart longing to relate in love to a people who refused to trust him. Does this ring a bell with you regarding your own personal life? It should, for all of us are pictured here.

To illustrate the correlation: Abraham and Sarah tried to help God out, since in their view he was unable to keep his promise to give them a son (read Genesis 16 & 17, Galatians 4:29–31). This is a picture of the flesh *in us,* with its inherent pride of achievement. The result, in their case, was a boy named Ishmael, the progenitor of the Arab peoples. It is most interesting to observe that the historic, and current, enmity between Arabs and Jews is a consequence of Abraham and Sarah's fleshly actions. Thus we see a pointed illustration of the consequences of the flesh—whether in them or in us.

The Second Look—The Gospels

In all the Old Testament history of Israel we see a thread of prophecy: Someone is coming! He will bring in better times. The Jews were looking for one called *"the Messiah."* So when we read the four Gospels, we see the focus on one person, Jesus, called the Christ (or *Messiah*). The gospel writers witness, *Here He Is!*

Not recognizing their Messiah, though given ample evidence, the Jews had him killed. In their mistaken religious zeal, they thought they were doing God a favor—to rid the world of this blasphemer. In doing so, they unconsciously fulfilled God's purpose, for Christ came to die for men's sins. But God raised him from the dead. Ever since, he has become the author of eternal life and salvation to *any* who want him to be their Lord, Jew or Gentile.

The Third Look—The Acts of the Apostles

A first century historian, Luke, recounts the history of God's new society, the church, in the Book of Acts. The unfolding action includes (1) the coming of the Holy Spirit to join all believers in Christ into one body, the church; (2) the early victories, problems, and persecution of Christians; (3) the ministry of the apostle Peter blending into that of the apostle Paul; and (4) concludes with Paul *"proclaiming the kingdom of God, and teaching concerning the Lord Jesus with all openness, unhindered"* (Acts 28:31 NASV). The action of this book is still going on. Its final chapters are, perhaps, being written in the life of the church today.

The Fourth Look—The Epistles

Even while he was engaged in his earthly ministry, the Lord Jesus laid the groundwork for this new society (see John 13 through 17). Thus, the men he called to begin the action he also prompted to write letters of instruction on how the new regime was to operate. So we have the New Testament letters.

The Fifth Look—The Revelation

The final book gives us the *Unveiling of Jesus Christ,* personally entering again into human history to set things right, to consummate man's day and to usher in eternity.

The whole of the biblical revelation, we observe, is centered around *one person*—Jesus Christ. So to summarize our panoramic view we can headline each section of scripture, as it relates to him, like this:

Jesus, the Messiah
⊤ *The Anticipation of His Coming—The Old Testament*
⊤ *The Realization of His Coming—The Gospels*

⊤ *The Presentation of His Message—The Acts of the Apostles*
⊤ *The Explanation of His Purposes—The New Testament Epistles*
⊤ *The Consummation of His Plan—The Revelation*

Here we have a simple example of the panoramic approach to Bible study. I suggest that you take a book of the Bible, perhaps one of the Gospels or the Book of Acts, and write your own synopsis of its contents, with a simple outline to summarize.

A real adventure is to make a New Testament survey, using this approach with every New Testament book. You'll never be the same if you do. My friend and colleague, Ray Stedman, has a tremendous grasp of the full scope of the biblical revelation. The following outline has resulted from his study. I think you'll find it highly instructive. But don't take his outline as final; work out your own from your personal grasp of the text of Scripture.

The Panorama of Scripture

THE GOAL—YOU—Complete in Christ.
Ephesians 4:11–13 and 2 Timothy 3:16,17

I. THE FUNCTION OF THE OLD TESTAMENT
Peculiar Purpose: Preparation, Anticipation:
to produce hunger,
to increase thirst.
An inescapable imperative to the understanding of truths of the New Testament.

A. FIVE BOOKS OF MOSES—(PENTATEUCH)
The *Pattern* of God's working.

GENESIS—Awakening Sense of Need	(HUMANITY)
EXODUS—New Relationship	(REDEMPTION)
LEVITICUS—New Resource	(ACCESS)
NUMBERS—Human Failure	(FLESH)
DEUTERONOMY—A New Law	(RESTORATION)

B. HISTORICAL BOOKS
The *Perils* of the Pathway.
JOSHUA—Peril of *premature contentment.*
Example of Grace—Joshua
JUDGES, RUTH—Peril of *consecrated ignorance.*
Example of Grace—Ruth
1 SAMUEL—Peril of *legalistic conformity and divided allegiance.*
Example of Grace—David and Jonathan
2 SAMUEL, 1 CHRONICLES—Peril of a *forgotten calling.*
Example of Grace—David's repentance.
1 KINGS, 2 CHRONICLES—Peril of *material magnificence and religious deceit.*
Example of Grace—Elijah
2 KINGS, 2 CHRONICLES—Peril of *moral abandonment and the hardened heart.*
Example of Grace—Hezekiah and Josiah
EZRA, NEHEMIAH, ESTHER—Peril of the *discouraged heart.*
Example of Grace—The personal life of each.

C. POETICAL BOOKS
The *Protests* of the Human Heart
JOB—(Cry of the Spirit) . . . . . . FAITH
PSALMS—(Cry of the Soul)
Voice of Emotions:
Yearning of Hope—Messianic
Burning of Anger—Imprecatory
Sighing of Sorrow—Penitential
Glorying of Grace—Victorious } HOPE
PROVERBS—(Cry of the Soul)
Expression of Mind
ECCLESIASTES—(Cry of the Soul)
Conclusion of the Will
SONG OF SOLOMON—(Cry of the Body) . . . LOVE

D. PROPHETIC BOOKS
The *Promises* of God. God offering Himself.
ISAIAH—Cleansing of God
JEREMIAH—Judgment of God
EZEKIEL—Presence of God
DANIEL—Mind of God
HOSEA—Persistence of God

JOEL—Ultimate Meaning
AMOS—Perfection
OBADIAH—Spiritual Victory
JONAH—Patience
MICAH—Pardon
NAHUM—Destruction
HABAKKUK—Ultimate Answers
ZEPHANIAH—Jealousy of God
HAGGAI—Integrity of God
ZECHARIAH—Encouragement
MALACHI—Responsibility of God

II. THE FUNCTION OF THE NEW TESTAMENT
Peculiar Purpose: Realization, Fulfillment:
to unveil Christ.

A. GOSPELS AND ACTS—The *Presentation* of Christ.
MATTHEW—Christ as King, proclaiming His Law.
MARK—Christ as Servant, ministering to a sick society.
LUKE—Christ as Man, praying—Man's lost secret.
JOHN—Christ as God, giving life—God's work.
ACTS—The Body of Christ—the unfinished book.

B. THE EPISTLES
The *Explanation* of Christ. Fall into three groups, each
group begun by a fundamental epistle (Romans, Ephesians, Hebrews.)

First Group—You in Christ
ROMANS—Panorama of Salvation (Key verse) 8:29–30
(3 tenses—*Justification, Sanctification, Glorification*)
1 CORINTHIANS—Fellowship with Christ   Key 1:9
Carnality—lack of fellowship
Spirituality—experience of fellowship
2 CORINTHIANS—Triumph in Christ   Key 2:14
Despite pressures—victory
GALATIANS—Freedom in Christ   Key 5:1
A red-hot "needle"

Second Group—Christ in You
EPHESIANS—The Nature of the Body   Key 2:19–20
PHILIPPIANS—The Problems of the Body   Key 2:5
COLOSSIANS—The Power of the Body   Key 3:3

THESSALONIANS—The Hope of the
  Body   Key I Th. 5:23–24
TIMOTHY—The Ministry of the Body   Key I Ti. 4:6
TITUS—The Work of the Body   Key 2:11–12
PHILEMON—The Unity of the Body

Third Group—Faith (the operative word)
HEBREWS—What Faith Is   Key 11:1
JAMES—What Faith Does   Key 2:26
PETER—Why Faith Suffers   Key I Peter 1:6–7
JOHN—How Faith Works   Key I John 3:23
JUDE—What Faith Faces   Key v. 3

C. REVELATION—The *Consummation* of Christ   Key 11:15

In the foregoing considerations, we have been concerned
mainly with *observation*. Now let's *interpret* and *apply* this
information. I conclude that *the centrality of the one person in
the whole Bible makes Jesus Christ the most important person there is,* in God's eyes. In application, I ask myself, what is
he to me? Is he the most important person in my life? Do I
really let him be Lord in my life in the practical level of making choices, determining life style and life direction? These
questions get pretty close to home, if he is as important as God
says he is. No wonder the Father said of him, *"This is my beloved Son, hear him!"*

The Telescopic View

To acquire a sound doctrinal base for Christian life we can
be greatly helped by topical studies. One way to engage in
such a study is this:

Procedure for Topical Study

  1. Select an interesting and important topic, such as "The
     Wrath of God."
  2. Without looking at your Bible or concordance, list the
     verses or Scripture portions on the subject that you

know, with references if possible. In other words, set down all that you know about the subject.

3. Take your concordance, subject index, topical or reference Bible, and count the references to this subject.
4. Look up each reference and list the ones that set forth a basic principle or key thought.
5. State these principles, that is, identify them by some pertinent phrase.
6. Track down the answers to any apparent contradictions so that you have an answer satisfying to you and one you can explain to others.
7. Write out the additional facts or facets of this subject that you learned in your study.
8. Note subjects that caught your interest, for future study.
9. Ask the Lord for an opportunity to share the truth learned.

Following this procedure on the subject, "The Wrath of God," I found my mind immediately recalled two verses, 1) "For the wrath of God is revealed from heaven against all ungodliness and unrighteousness of men, who suppress the truth in unrighteousness" (Rom. 1:18 NASV) and 2) "For God has not destined us for wrath, but for obtaining salvation through Jesus Christ our Lord" (1 Thess. 5:9 NASV).

Not bad for a starter, I thought, until I went from there to Strong's *Exhaustive Concordance* and found some 208 references to *wrath*. I got less than one per cent. Keeping in mind that Strong's Concordance lists the references in the King James version, I sorted out those which referred to *God's* wrath and found there were 140. Of these, 105 were in the Old Testament and 35 in the New Testament. It's not hard to see why people see the God of the Old Testament as a God of wrath, while the God of the New Testament appears to be a God of love. But he's the same God! He has not changed; he has always been a God of love *and* wrath, for if he didn't love us he would not get angry about that which hurts us. But here

I am moving into the interpretation realm, perhaps prematurely, so let's get back to our observations.

Scanning through the Old Testament references on the subject, I make the general observation that God's wrath was turned on his people because of their strong-willed disobedience and idolatry, but was always redemptive, not punitive, in nature. Isaiah characterizes God's wrath *toward his own* in these words:

> For a brief moment I forsook you, but with great compassion I will gather you. In overflowing wrath for a moment I hid my face from you, but with everlasting love I will have compassion on you, says the Lord, your Redeemer (Isa. 54:7, 8).

and he adds:

> For the mountains may depart and the hills be removed, but my steadfast love shall not depart from you . . . (Isa. 54:10).

But regarding Ammon, the entrenched enemy of God and his people, he says:

> A sword, a sword is drawn for the slaughter . . . to be laid to the necks of the unhallowed wicked, whose day has come, the time of their final punishment . . . you shall be no more remembered; for I the Lord have spoken (Ezek. 21:28, 29 & 32).

No such statements are issued against God's own people, only against those who refuse him and steadfastly oppose his will. The prophet Habakkuk knew this about his God, for he said to the Lord, *". . . in wrath remember mercy"* (Hab. 3:2).

Moving to the New Testament data, we see the picture rounding out: mercy is always there for those who will turn back to God in the obedience of faith.

> He who believes in the Son has eternal life; he who does not obey the Son shall not see life, but the wrath of God rests on him (John 3:36).

> Do you not know that God's kindness is meant to lead you to repentance? But by your hard and impenitent heart you are

storing up wrath for yourself on the day of wrath when God's righteous judgment shall be revealed (Rom. 2:4, 5).

So we observe that there are two possibilities: either we are storing up wrath through our unbelief and disobedience, or we are enjoying life in Christ through our faith in him and obedience to his Word.

As we pursue our investigation to the end of the story, we find in the Book of Revelation the final expression of God's wrath. There are those in that day who would prefer to be buried by an avalanche rather than to repent. They say to the mountains and rocks, "Fall on us and hide us from the face of him who is seated on the throne, and from the wrath of the Lamb . . ." (Rev. 6:16). The wrath of a lamb? Who ever heard of a fearsome lamb? This paradox of terms says a lot: "the Lamb of God" who has taken away men's sins is descriptive of the redemptive nature of our God; but having refused him in this character, he becomes an awesome one whose wrath is to be feared.

The final word on God's wrath is this:

. . . he will tread the wine press of the fury of the wrath of God the Almighty. On his robe and on his thigh he has a name inscribed, King of kings and Lord of lords (Rev. 19:15, 16).

The Lamb is Lord over all, and those who oppose his gracious reign have only his wrath left to face. Yet even after this word of impending judgment, there comes the gracious invitation, ". . . let him who is thirsty come, let him who desires take the water of life without price" (Rev. 22:17). Even in this awesome time of the final expression of his wrath, God remembers mercy. What a great and gracious God!

Note that we have mingled observation and interpretation in running through the verses on God's wrath. We do this almost unconsciously, as we absorb the content of the scripture and think through its meaning. Now let's try to identify some principles regarding this subject. Here are some that occurred to me:

1. *God's wrath is not directed at people* so much as it is against their conduct in opposition to his will and way.
2. *People only experience God's wrath when they refuse to obey God's Word.*
3. *In relation to God's wrath, there are two classes of people,* a) those who are related to God as his people by faith, to whom God's wrath becomes corrective and redemptive, and b) those who refuse to relate to God in love, and thus inherit the folly of their own stubborn, willful opposition to God, in the experience of his wrath. This, for them, means utter destruction, for one cannot defy the living God in his sovereign authority (see 2 Thess. 1:7–10).
4. According to Romans 1:18 *the wrath of God is now being revealed* in the present mess the world is in. Three times in this chapter we read "God gave them up" (Rom. 1:24, 26, and 28). In essence God says, "Since you don't want *my* way I'll give you over to your own way that you may learn to value my way." This is the present expression of God's wrath. *But there is a future expression of his wrath* from which there is no recovery. Meanwhile, he is longsuffering toward us, that his goodness may lead us to repentance.
5. *God's heart is always redemptive,* but salvation refused leaves only God's righteous wrath against sin to be visited on the sinner.
6. *God's wrath is to be avoided* at all costs. The price of disobedience is too high.

   Thank God "he has delivered us from the dominion of darkness and transferred us to the kingdom of his beloved Son, in whom we have redemption, the forgiveness of sins" (Col. 1:13, 14).
7. There is no need for anyone to feel the weight of God's wrath. He sent a Savior. "For God sent the Son into the world, not to condemn the world, but that the world

might be saved through him. He who believes in him is not condemned; he who does not believe is condemned already, because he has not believed in the name of the only Son of God" (John 3:17, 18).

So I conclude that God is not a petulant, vindictive, or punitive deity just waiting to catch us in some failure, but rather he is a loving, kind, heavenly Father committed to achieving nothing but the best for his children—even if they must have a spanking. He is, on the other hand, utterly righteous, and will not change the way things are in his sovereign order just because we don't want to conform to his plan.

"God is love" (1 John 4:8). But he is also *"a consuming fire"* (Heb. 12:29). Such a one is to be loved and obeyed—not to be taken lightly or presumed upon.

In working through this topical study, I have carefully followed the procedure outlined at the beginning. You can identify the steps if you think it through. The only point I did not address is to note subjects that caught my interest. To consider this item, all the way through my study I kept thinking I must now study the other side of the picture, the *grace* of God. With this additional study, I will hopefully achieve a balanced view of two vital topics centering around *the character of God.* Such study can bring nothing but profit.

The Microscopic View

Now we come to what, in my opinion, is the most productive approach to Bible study, the detailed, analytical look. Once again, some steps on how to proceed in this investigative adventure may be useful.

Let's start with a simple approach to the study of a single verse of scripture, or a short passage.

Discovering God's Truth

1. Seeing the Setting   (*reconnaissance*)
2. Pulling into Focus   (*observation*)

3. Getting on Target   (*meditation*)
4. Hitting the Bullseye   (*interpretation*)
5. Getting the Point   (*application*)
6. Putting It Back Together   (*outlining*)

I suggest you take six blank sheets of paper and write in headings with spaces in between as we have done on the following pages:

DISCOVERING GOD'S TRUTH

Step I

Seeing the Setting   (Reconnaissance)

a. From the **Local Scene:**

b. From the **Broader View:** other scripture, history, the whole Bible.

CHAPTER 4

THEN Jesus was led up by the Spirit into the wildern
the devil.

2 And after He had fasted forty days and forty nigl
hungry.

3 And the tempter came and said to Him, "If You
command that these stones become bread."

4 But He answered and "It is written, 'MA
BREAD ALONE ON EVERY THAT PROCEEDS OU
GOD.'"

5 The *took into the holy city; a
the pinnacle ple,

6 and *sa n, " u are the Son of God t
for it is written,

'HE ANGELS CHARGE CONCERNING
And HANDS THEY WILL BEAR YOU U
LE YOUR FOOT AGAINST A STONE.'

7 O her hand, it is wri
10TEMP

gai Hi to a very high mo
Him and the kingdoms the world, and their glory;

9 and he said to Him, "All these things will I give
and worship me

10 Then Jesus *said to him, "Begone, Satan! Fo
SHALL WORSHIP THE LORD YOUR GOD, AND SERVE HIM ON

11 Then the devil *left Him; and behold, angels
minister to Him.

12 Now when He heard that John had been take
withdrew into Galilee;

13 and leaving Nazareth, He came and settled in (
by the sea, in the region of Zebulun and Naphtali.

14 This was to fulfill what was spoken through
saying,

DISCOVERING GOD'S TRUTH

Step 2

Pulling into Focus   **(Observation)**

Observe What It Says, one word at a time!

DISCOVERING GOD'S TRUTH

Step 3

Getting on Target   **(Meditation)**

Decide What It Means, weighing possible alternatives:

DISCOVERING GOD'S TRUTH

Step 4

Hitting the Bullseye   **(Interpretation)**

Draw Conclusions:
  a. In statement of principles.

  b. What's the big idea?

DISCOVERING GOD'S TRUTH

Step 5

Getting the Point   **(Application)**

Determine "How it affects me," and "What must I do about it?"

DISCOVERING GOD'S TRUTH

Step 6

Putting It Back Together   (Outlining)

Well . . . you did pretty well at taking it apart, now see if you can put it together again!
Schematic Summary (sometimes called an outline)

Final Exam: Will it hold together?

Now choose a single verse of scripture and fill out the blank spaces concerning your chosen text. I've done it with a most interesting verse, Isaiah 53:11. On the next seven pages (84–90) you can see what I have done as a sample, then do likewise with your own subject. Here's the text I have chosen to analyze:

> He shall see the fruit of the travail
>   of his soul and be satisfied;
> by his knowledge shall the righteous
>   one, my servant,
> make many to be accounted righteous;
>   and he shall bear their iniquities (Isa. 53:11).

DISCOVERING GOD'S TRUTH—STEP 1

Seeing the Setting   **(Reconnaissance)**
  around Isaiah 53:11

a. **From the Local Scene:**

   1. *The chapter, back to 52:13 is a remarkable pro-phetic picture of the atoning work of Christ.*
   2. *The immediate context portrays the value of his death, and resurrection.*
   3. *The book (and passage) is Isaiah's prophecy addressed to Israel. The passage presents Israel's redeemer.*

b. **From the Broader View: other scripture, history, the whole Bible.**

   1. *Probably the clearest exposition in Old Testament or New Testament of the value of the atoning work of Christ.*
   2. *Prophetic portrait of Christ as the suffering servant of Jehovah, written 700 B.C.*
   3. *Text and early date confirmed by two manuscripts dated second century B.C. found among Dead Sea Scrolls.*
   4. *So extensive is his writing concerning the person and work of Christ that Isaiah has been called the Evangelical Prophet.*

DISCOVERING GOD'S TRUTH—STEP 2

about Isaiah 53:11

Pulling into Focus   **(Observation)**

Observe What It Says, *one word at a time!*

He shall see—He (the Lord Jesus)
   shall see (after death—RESURRECTION)
   see—in the sense of perceiving after observation.
   (Declaration of fact)

The fruit—the result

of His travail—resulting from as a source.
   travail—more than physical suffering, includes "being made sin" and experiencing the separation from the Father that this entails.

of His soul—relating to His perfect, sinless humanity.

and be satisfied—The consequence of His seeing.
   Satisfied—feeling that it was all worth the cost, finding no fault with the Father's will.

by His knowledge—i.e., the knowledge of Him.

the righteous one—Christ, the one absolutely right, without fault or flaw.

my servant—Jehovah, speaking of Christ as obedient unto death.

DISCOVERING GOD'S TRUTH—STEP 2, Cont'd.

make many—*He will do it for many (i.e. all who receive Him)*

to be accounted righteous—*this is justification. Those who know Him shall be declared blameless of sin through His righteousness.*
Accounted—*it's God's accounting.*

and—*"for" of KJV is better, as explanatory clause as to how He will make many to be accounted righteous.*

He shall bear—*Christ shall (the passage is prophetic) bear, i.e. carry, take on Himself as His burden.*

their—*the "many"*

iniquities—*wickedness, gross injustice, unrighteousness*

DISCOVERING GOD'S TRUTH—STEP 3

Getting on Target   **(Meditation)**
    about Isaiah 53:11

Decide What It Means, weighing possible alternatives:

1. *There is a question regarding the antecedents of the pronouns: I take it that this is saying that* <u>Christ</u> *is satisfied with the results of His sacrifice.*

   I see no <u>strong</u> *reason why it could not equally well be that* <u>God</u> *is satisfied.*

2. *This is* <u>justification by faith</u> *in the Old Testament. It means that:*

   a. *Christ* <u>shall be satisfied with the results of His sacrifice.</u>

   b. *Through the* <u>knowledge of Christ many shall be accounted righteous because Christ has borne their sins.</u>

DISCOVERING GOD'S TRUTH—STEP 4

Hitting the Bullseye   **(Interpretation)**
   on Isaiah 53:11

Draw Conclusions:

a. In statement of Principles.

1. Justification is through the knowledge of Christ as the atoning sacrifice for sins.

2. The Lord Jesus is satisfied with the result of His atoning work on the cross.

3. Christ is <u>alive,</u> enjoying the result of His obedience.

b. What's the Big Idea?

Really two ideas:

1. <u>The satisfaction of Christ</u> with His work.

2. <u>The justification of believers,</u> those who know Him as sin-bearer.

DISCOVERING GOD'S TRUTH—STEP 5

Getting the Point   **(Application)**
    of Isaiah 53:11

Determine How it affects me, and What must I do about it?

1. *Since Christ is satisfied with His atoning work, certainly I should be.*

2. *I am accounted righteous through what He has done in my behalf.*

3. *He bore MY iniquities—hence I don't have to bear them. This means freedom from guilt.*

4. *ONE sin-bearer is enough!*
   I must not harbor sins that Christ has dealt with in Himself.

DISCOVERING GOD'S TRUTH—STEP 6

Putting It Back Together   **(Outlining)**

Well . . . you did pretty well at taking it apart, now see if you can put it together again!

Schematic Summary (sometimes called an outline)
   of Isaiah 53:11

   A. *The SAVIOR'S SATISFACTION*
         vs. 11a

   B. *The SINNERS' JUSTIFICATION*
         vs. 11b

Final Exam: Will it hold together?
   Yes, I think I've got the message.

Taking another passage, this time three verses from the New Testament, here's another sample study on Ephesians 2:8–10.

For by grace you have been saved through faith; and this is not your own doing, it is the gift of God—not because of works, lest any man should boast. For we are his workmanship, created in Christ Jesus for good works, which God prepared beforehand, that we should walk in them (Eph. 2:8–10).

My study of these verses follows on the next seven pages (93–99):

DISCOVERING GOD'S TRUTH—STEP 1

Seeing the Setting   **(Reconnaissance)**
about Ephesians 2:8–10

a. From the **Local Scene**:

In a chapter describing
What we were vs. what we are in Christ.

In a book—which is a letter written by Paul to the Christians at Ephesus (& everywhere) telling God's purposes in placing us together in Christ as members of His body, the Church.

b. From the **Broader View**: other Scripture, history, the whole **Bible**.

Historical background—Acts 19

Doctrinal correlation—see Acts 4:12, 15:8–11, 13: 38, 39
Romans 4:4, 5, 16–21, 10:34, 11:6, 5:8
Titus 3:3–8

Bible Orientation—Presents the Church as Christ's body, companion to Colossians, which presents Christ as Head over the body.

This passage highlights the work of God in taking poor material and making it fit for His use and habitation.

DISCOVERING GOD'S TRUTH—STEP 2
about Ephesians 2:8–10

Pulling into Focus   **(Observation)**

Observe What It Says, one word at a time!

v.8   *For*—Explanatory of preceding

      by grace—God's undeserved favor, doing for us what we do not deserve and could not do for ourselves.

      you have been—present perfect tense, indicates accomplished fact being currently experienced.

      saved—rescued, made whole, conserved for intended use.

      (This statement is a DECLARATION OF FACT)

      through faith—channel or medium of application or reception—modifying phrase

      and this—this what? faith or salvation? *What is faith?*

      *is not your own doing—modifying clause explanatory of main proposition

      it is the Gift of God—DECLARATION OF FACT

v.9   **not because of works*—further explanatory phrase, limiting proposition.

      *lest any man should boast—added modifying clause further limiting main statement of fact. God does it, no ground to boast.

DISCOVERING GOD'S TRUTH—STEP 2, Cont'd

v.10 <u>For</u>—*explanatory again*

> <u>we are His workmanship</u>—*another DECLARA-*
> *TION OF FACT the product of His working.*

> <u>created</u>—*again the work of God, the Creator*

> <u>in Christ Jesus</u>—*the sphere of our life; we are a*
> *new creation in Him.*

> <u>for good works</u>—*the end for which He made us*
> *anew.*

> **<u>which God has prepared beforehand</u>—explana-*
> *tory clause, modifying main statement. Not just*
> *<u>any</u> good works, but according to God's previ-*
> *ous planning.*

> <u>that we should walk in them</u>—*purpose clause. This*
> *should be the pattern of our life and conduct,*
> *doing what He has planned for us.*

*   * modify main declaration of fact*

DISCOVERING GOD'S TRUTH—STEP 3

Getting on Target   **(Meditation)**
    about Ephesians 2:8–10

Decide What It Means, weighing possible alternatives:

1. *We who are Christians have been saved by God alone, apart from any work or effort on our own part. God has done all that is possible and necessary for salvation.*

2. *Salvation is received through faith. Faith is taking God at His word, that is, believing what He has said is true and acting upon it. Faith is not the gift, salvation is. God commands men to "believe on the Lord Jesus." Man has the capacity to obey or disobey this command. The Gospel is a valid proposition—addressed to faith, demanding a response from the will of man.*

3. *Good works are God's intent for man, and the result of saving faith in Christ. These works are not done independently of God, but are the result of and empowered by His working in us (we are His workmanship).*

4. *God has a plan for us. A specific pattern of good works plotted out for us. Our place is to discover (a step at a time) what He has for us to do, and DO it.*

DISCOVERING GOD'S TRUTH—STEP 4

Hitting the Bullseye   **(Interpretation)**
   re: Ephesians 2:8–10

Draw Conclusions:

a. In statement of PRINCIPLES.

1. Salvation is an accomplished fact and a present reality for those who are Christ's.

2. It is a gift, received by faith.

3. God's unmerited favor toward us is its source.

4. Salvation is not achieved by man's works.

5. Salvation does not originate with man.

6. Good works are the consequence of our belonging to God.

7. God has a prearranged plan for our life.

b. What's the BIG IDEA?

THIS IS AN EXPLANATION OF THE TRUTH CONCERNING OUR SALVATION IN CHRIST.

DISCOVERING GOD'S TRUTH—STEP 5

Getting the Point   **(Application)**
of Ephesians 2:8–10

Determine "How it affects me," and "What must I do about it?"

1. *I have made, and can make, no contribution toward my personal salvation. All I can do is to take the great gift of grace that God offers in His Son.*

2. *Any attempts at self-justification or claims of self-righteousness are a contradiction of the truth of this passage. My complete dependence should thus be on Jesus Christ.*

3. *I must allow God to go on working in me as "His workmanship."*

4. *I must seek to discover and walk in the specific plan of God for my life.*

DISCOVERING GOD'S TRUTH—STEP 6

Putting It Back Together   **(Outlining)**

Well . . . you did pretty well at taking it apart, now see if you can put it together again!

Schematic Summary (sometimes called an outline)
   of Ephesians 2:8–10

Our Salvation

A. *A Settled State*
   1. An accomplished fact   *2:8a*
   2. A present experience

B. *A Sovereign Source*
   1. Completely from God
   2. Not from human origin or works   *2:8b–9*

C. *A Prearranged Purpose*
   1. Arranged by God   *2:10*
   2. Performed by us.

D. *A Calculated Condition*
   *Faith. God is not content to be cut out of our lives in
         any degree.   2:8a*

Final Exam: Will it hold together?
   Sure think so!

Another Method

There is another plan for employing the microscopic approach to Bible study, probably more usable on a larger segment of scripture than the approach we have just considered. It is this:

Procedure for Analytical Study

1. Choose a portion of Scripture on which you would like to have additional light.

Read it over several times, in different versions if possible.

2. Look for the central thought and write it down.

Divide into natural paragraphs and give each division a title.

3. Look up definitions and derivations of the important words (use dictionaries).

Phrase or re-phrase these definitions in terms that you understand. Simplify the dictionary definition if possible.

4. Observe the most frequently used words or phrases to determine the emphasis or thrust.

5. Trace through the argument or progress of thought of the writer and think through the steps used in arriving at a conclusion.

6. Make your own paraphrased translation of the passage in contemporary American language. This will show you just how much you really understand of the passage, and will enable you to transmit the truth you have learned to someone else, in terms easy to understand.

Choose a Passage and Read It

Let's try it on Colossians 3. Having made this choice, I read it through in the Revised Standard Version, the New American Standard, the New English Bible, the New International New Testament, the Amplified New Testament, the Living Bible, the King James Version, and finally a Greek-English interlinear translation.

Central Thought and Divisions

As I did so, the central thought, or theme, I perceived was "God's Design for Godly Living." The paragraph breaks I observed are these, with appropriate titles:
1. New Life in Christ 3:1, 4
2. Taking Off Our Old Dirty Clothes 3:5–11
3. Putting On New Garments 3:12–4:6
   a. In general conduct 3:12–17
   b. In marriage 3:18, 19
   c. In child/parent relationships 3:20, 21
   d. In slave/master relationships 3:22–4:1
   e. In regard to prayer 4:2–4
      1) In general 4:2
      2) In intercession for others 4:3, 4
   f. In relation to worldlings 4:5, 6
      1) In wisdom, redeeming opportunities 4:5
      2) In gracious (not insipid) speech 4:6

Note that I ignored the chapter break, since it does not accord with the thought content.

Definitions of Words

My study of words gave me the following, working from the verse order of the Revised Standard Version:

put to death = believe that we died with Christ to the power of sin (understood in this context).
immorality = fornication, sexual sin.
impurity = moral uncleanness
passion = lustful desire
evil desire = a craving for bad things

covetousness = greediness
idolatry = worshipping things that are seen
wrath = anger (in context, God's righteous anger)
anger = (in context, on man's part) slow-burning revengeful
   attitude
malice = just plain badness
slander = injurious speech
foul talk = obscene language
old nature = old man (as I was in Adam)
new nature = new man (as I am in Christ)
image = a visible representation of a prototype
circumcised = a term equivalent to "the Jews"
uncircumcised = a term equivalent to "the Gentiles"
barbarian = a comparative term: the more crude type of people
Scythian = from their reputation: the very worst sort
compassion = heart concern for the problems of others
kindness = committed to practical help, good heartedness
lowliness = willingness to take the humble place
meekness = power under control
patience = able to take abuse without losing your cool
forebearing = putting up with people the way they are
rule = mediate, arbitrate
admonish = to call to mind, for warning or encouragement
be subject = to rank under, take second place
love = commitment of the will to act in a way that will serve
   another
be harsh = be bitter, irritate
obey = to hear under authority
provoke = exasperate
eye service = working only when the boss is looking
men-pleasers = seeking human approval
singleness of heart = aiming to please one Lord
fearing (the Lord) = caring first and foremost what the Lord
   thinks and says

reward = to give as a result of a relationship (in this context)
inheritance = what the Father leaves to his children
mystery = a revealed secret, to those in the know, taught by
   God
wisely = properly using that which you know
outsiders = those not yet in Christ
gracious = with kindness and good will
seasoned with salt = to give taste and zest to that which could
   be flat and insipid

I derived these definitions by consulting Vine's *Expository Dictionary of New Testament Words,* working through the King James Version words to the Revised Standard Version, then adding my own flavor to the definition from my own understanding of the words in American vernacular terms. Yes, it was a lot of work—but worth it, for now I have a much clearer understanding of what this passage is all about.

Most Frequent Usage

Observing the most frequently used words to determine emphasis, I found that the thrust of the passage was centered around "putting off and putting on." *Put to death* (v. 5), *put them all away* (v. 8), *put off* (v. 9), *put on* (v. 10), *put on* (v. 12), and *put on* (v. 14) all reflect this idea.

Grammatically, the series of imperatives makes strong impact.

♦ *Set your minds on things above!*
♦ *Put to death what is earthly in you!*
♦ *Put them all away* (those evil things)!
♦ *Put off the old man!*
♦ *Put on the new man!*
♦ *Put on then as God's chosen ones* (all these graces of spirit)!

♦ *And above all put on love!*
♦ *Let the peace of Christ rule in your hearts!*
♦ *Be thankful!*
♦ *Let the word of Christ dwell in you!*
♦ *Do everything in the name of the Lord Jesus!*
♦ *Wives, be subject to your husbands!*
♦ *Husbands, love your wives!*
♦ *Children, obey your parents!*
♦ *Fathers, do not provoke your children!*
♦ *Slaves, obey your earthly masters!*
♦ *Masters, treat your slaves justly and fairly!*
♦ *Continue steadfast in prayer!*
♦ *Pray for us!*
♦ *Conduct yourselves wisely toward outsiders!*
♦ *Let your speech be always with grace!*

Some impact, when you consider each of these is a demand upon our will—to *do* it! This makes it even more imperative that we *"put on the Lord Jesus Christ,* and make no provision for the flesh, to gratify its desires," as we have it in Romans 13:14. He is the one who enables us to do all the rest, as we trust him.

Tracing the Argument

As I trace through the progress of thought of the writer, his argument seems clear. Since we have the risen Christ, and he is our life; and since he has the place of honor and authority; and since we died with him and now our life is hid with him in God; and since we share his glory (all in verses 1–4 of chapter 3), we have no need to live in the old way. We *can* now, because of all these facts, put off the old life and adopt a new life style consistent with the one who is our life, the Lord Jesus. All the commands and exhortations that follow are based on this premise. The rest of the passage is just

telling us what we must put off and what we must put on—
God's new design for living. This is spelled out in generalities,
applicable to all Christians, then in specifics relating to the
various relationships of life. It concludes with instructions
about how we should talk to God and how we should talk to
men.

Your Own Paraphrased Translation

There is just one more step in our procedure: to make our
own translation in paraphrased form, using our own terms. So
here it is—Colossians 3:1 to 4:6, my version:

(3:1) Therefore, since you were raised together with Christ,
seek the things above, where Christ is sitting at God's right hand.
Stop being preoccupied with earthly things. For you died, and your
life is centered in Christ and is being kept with Christ in God;
whenever Christ, our life, shall be made evident, then also you
will be shown to be with him in the splendor of his character.

(3:5) Therefore, put to death that which belongs to your
strictly human, earthly ways: the improper use of sex, moral uncleanness, lustful desires and urges, craving for evil things, and
greediness, which is worshiping material things (instead of the living God). Because of these things in which you formerly walked,
the righteous anger of God is coming, yes, because of these things
in which you once lived.

(3:8) But now put away all these: revengeful anger, ill will,
injurious talk about others, and foul, obscene language coming
out of your mouth. Stop lying to each other, having put off the old
man with his habits, and having put on the new man, who has
been renewed in fuller knowledge to conform to the likeness of the
one who created this new man. In him there is no place for human
differences of status, whether national, religious, cultural, or social;
rather Christ is all that matters, and in all his people.

(3:12) Therefore, all of you, as God's chosen ones, devoted to
his own special purposes and dearly loved by him, put on (as you
would a fresh, clean garment) these life qualities: a deep heart-
concern for the needs of others, good-heartedness that makes you
of down-to-earth usefulness, a genuine willingness (having thought
it through) to take the humble place, soft courage which is neither

inflated by praise nor resentful of injury, a steadiness under provocation that keeps you from having a short fuse, a patient acceptant attitude which enables you to put up with people the way they are, a forgiving heart (for if anyone has a complaint against another, you must forgive—just as the Lord has forgiven you. Remember?)

(3:14) The overriding principle over all these things is love, the kind that knocks itself out for the loved one and never quits. This is the quality that holds it all together and shows how mature we really are.

And let the peace which Christ wrought be the mediator in your hearts, to which you were surely called in the one body—*his* body; and be thankful.

(3:16) Let the word of Christ make its home in you richly: teaching, warning and encouraging each other from it, applying the truth wisely—singing in psalms, in hymns and in spiritual songs with thanks in your hearts to God; and whatever you do, in your words and in your work, do everything in the character and authority of the Lord Jesus, giving thanks to God the Father through him.

(3:18) You wives, be subject to your husbands (that is, put him first), for this fits the Lord's plan. You husbands, love your wives (with the same kind of love with which God loves you—which means putting her first), and don't be caustic toward them. You children, listen to your parents and heed them, for this pleases the Lord greatly. You fathers, don't exasperate your children, or you will turn them off. You slaves, hear your masters as under their authority in everything; they are your lords in a human sense. Obey them, not just when they are watching, just to please them, but with unmixed motives caring *most* about what the Lord thinks and says.

(3:23) Whatever you do, do your work from the heart, as to the Lord and not to men, knowing that you will receive from the Lord that which he gives back to you in your inheritance, given because you are his child. You serve the LORD Christ.

(3:25) Surely the one acting unjustly will bring on himself what he did wrong, and there is no partiality in this. You masters extend to your slaves that which is just and fair, knowing that you also have a Lord in heaven.

(4:2) Be persistently engaged in prayer, being alive to its potential, with thanksgiving; also praying together about us, that God may open a door for us to tell the sacred secret, now revealed, about Christ, because of which I am in bonds, that I may make it clear as I ought.

(4:5) Conduct yourselves wisely toward those who are not yet in God's family, using every opportunity with them, your speech always being gracious, having been seasoned with salt and thus not flat and insipid, to know how you ought to answer each one.

Now Interpret

Since we have now done a pretty thorough observation of the text, our next step is to deal with the interpretive problems and arrive at conclusions—then to apply the truth learned. I expect by now you can do this for yourself, using the principles we have suggested earlier. So, to avoid being tedious, I will only touch on some of the interpretive areas as examples, rather than try to interpret the whole passage for you.

The first interpretive decision I faced is in Colossians 3:4. Here I had to decide whether Paul was referring to the future coming of Christ or his present manifestation in the believer. For at least two reasons I chose the latter, (1) because the context is dealing with present conduct, not future conditions, and (2) because the word *when* in verse 4 is really *whenever* in the Greek text (I admit I may have an advantage over you if you do not have access to the Greek, but you can get a Greek-English interlinear translation like I have and read it right out of that in English). The point is, I believe, that since Christ is our life, as we walk with him our life will be evidencing the glory of his character. What a delightful prospect! No wonder Paul adds, "Therefore put to death your human, earthly ways . . ." which characterized your former way of life without Christ.

This correlates with my understanding of the meaning of ". . . do everything in the name of the Lord Jesus," in verse 17. To act *in the name of* another is to act out of his authority and consistent with his character and purposes—just as if it were that person acting. We are truly *his representatives* among men! How important, then, the impression we convey to a watching world.

Verse 25 of Chapter 3, I decided, goes with the instruction to masters in 4:1, not with the preceding section, which properly ends with the emphatic "You serve the Lord Christ." Here the emphasis is clearly on the word *Lord,* as having the right to exercise authority over us. But it also uses the rather unusual combination of terms in *the Lord Christ,* instead of the usual expression, *the Lord Jesus.* The word *Christ* means "anointed one," that is "one empowered and able to do a job," so here we have the lordship of Jesus (with its right to demand obedience from us) coupled with his ability to supply all we need to fulfill those demands. This, to me, is an interesting and pointed use of our Lord's names, interpretively very significant.

And Apply . . .

The applications are many if I take the passage in detail—and you can make your own as the Lord points you to an area of need. But in general, the passage says to us that it really matters what life style we adopt, for we are accountable to the Lord Christ. Since he is our *life,* what we do and say every day reflects on him, whether favorably or unfavorably. So I need to be consistently *putting off* the old ways and *putting on* the Lord Jesus—to show forth that newness of life I have in him. But this is not some legalistic paste-on, rather it is just being myself *in Christ* and allowing his life to show through in all that I do.

Through this study, I was greatly encouraged to keep responding to Jesus Christ as my Lord. Though it took some time and work on my part, I'm glad I did it. Please note that what I have suggested to you in study procedures I have done myself, so if you think I've made it too tough on you, at least you can't say I'm not fair about it.

This chapter concludes Phase 1, the basics of Bible inter-pretation. I hope you find it helpful and sufficiently rewarding to move to Phase 2, a study of Figurative Language.

Phase 2

Figurative Language

□ 7 □

Figures of Speech

One of the most enlightening aspects of language is the study of figurative expressions.

Milton Terry introduces us to this subject with keen insight:

> The natural operations of the human mind prompt men to trace analogies and make comparisons. Pleasing emotions are excited and the imagination is gratified by the use of metaphors and similes. Were we to suppose a language sufficiently copious in words to express all possible conceptions, the human mind would still require us to compare and contrast our concepts, and such a procedure would soon necessitate a variety of figures of speech. So much of our knowledge is acquired through the senses, that all our abstract ideas and our spiritual language have a material base. "It is not too much to say," observes Max Muller, "that the whole dictionary of ancient religion is made up of metaphors. With us these metaphors are all forgotten. We speak of *spirit* without thinking of *breath,* of *heaven* without thinking of *sky,* of *pardon* without thinking of a *release,* of *revelation* without thinking of a *veil.* But in ancient language every one of these words, nay, every word that does not refer to sensuous objects, is still in a chrysalis stage, half material and half spiritual, and rising and falling in its character according to the capacities of its speakers and hearers." [1]

---

[1] Milton S. Terry, *Biblical Hermeneutics* (Grand Rapids: Zondervan Publishing House, n.d.), p. 244.

What potent possibilities, then, lie in concepts conveyed by figurative language! So, moving to specifics, let's explore the various figures of speech. I'll list some of them, along with illustrations of their use on the following pages.

Figures of Speech

SIMILE (*similis* = like)	A formal comparison using "*as . . . so*" or "*like*" to express resemblance. "*Even so*, husbands should love their own wives *as* their own bodies . . .*" (Eph. 5:28).
METAPHOR (*Meta + phero* = a carrying over)	An implied comparison, a word applied to something it is not, to suggest a resemblance. "*Benjamin is a ravenous wolf . . .*" (Gen. 49:27).
IRONY (*Eiron* = a dissembling speaker)	The speaker or writer says the very opposite of what he intends to convey. ". . . *you are the people and wisdom will die with you*" (Job 12:1).
METONYMY (*Meta + onoma* = a change of name)	One word is used in place of another to portray some actual relationship between the things signified. "*Kill the passover . . .*" (Exod. 12:21 KJV) where the paschal lamb is meant.
HYPERBOLE (*Huper + bole* = a throwing beyond)	Intentional exaggeration for the purpose of emphasis, or a magnifying beyond reality. "*If your right eye causes you to sin, pluck it out and throw it away . . .*" (Matt. 5:29).
PERSONIFICATION (To make like a person)	Inanimate objects are spoken of as persons, as if they had life. "*The sea looked and fled . . .*" (Ps. 114:3,4).
APOSTROPHE (*apo + strepho* = to turn from)	Turning from the immediate hearers to address an absent or imaginary person or thing. "*Ah, sword of the Lord! How long till you are quiet?*" (Jer. 47:6).
SYNECDOCHE (*sun + ekdechomai* to receive from and associate with)	Where the whole is put for a part, or a part for the whole, an individual for a class and vice-versa. "*And we were in all 276 souls . . .*" in Acts 27:37, where *soul* is used for the whole person.

Simile

First, let's compare simile and metaphor. Ephesians 5:22 –
27 is a simile, making a formal comparison between Christ
and the church on the one hand, and husbands and wives on
the other. The words "as . . . so" or "even so" make this
very clear. And this figure heightens our interest and dignifies
the marriage relationship, especially if we see it in outline
form, like this:

(AS) with CHRIST AND THE CHURCH	(SO) with HUSBANDS AND WIVES
CHRIST LOVED THE CHURCH and gave HIMSELF up for her . . . Eph. 5:25	*HUSBANDS, LOVE your WIVES as CHRIST LOVED the CHURCH . . .* Eph 5:25
"THAT he might sanctify her" (Eph. 5:26) i.e. that we might be put to the intended use for which he created us: a) as an expression of his own *LIFE* and *CHARACTER.* b) to fulfill our calling, enjoy our God-given ministries. c) and much more (you add the rest.)	THAT the husband might sanctify his wife. i.e. that she might SHARE HIS LIFE, be his helper, etc. a) expressing her own personality and life in Christ. b) employing her gifts in a spiritual ministry. c) be the *ruler* of the *home*, in all that means to her husband and children.
"THAT he might present the church to himself in splendor" (Eph. 5:27) i.e. that he might enjoy the benefits stemming from his unselfish love— in enjoying his Bride. And lead us on to the fulfillment of our manhood and womanhood by his love.	THAT the husband might seek his wife's fulfillment, and enjoy her. i.e. that he may enjoy the beauty and glory of her fulfilled womanhood, as he undertakes the responsibility of his headship—leading her with the leadership of love to ultimate fulfillment.
"THAT she might be holy and without blemish" (Eph. 5:27). i.e. that his work in us may go on to completion, that we may be wholly his.	THAT the husband be faithful, hanging in there. i.e. that his commitment may be steadfast and permanent, in spite of problems.
"Having cleansed her by *the washing of water with the word"* (Eph. 5:26) Based on *COMMUNICATION* which his loving heart initiates—to keep us close, mutually enjoying our love relationship.	Husbands are to keep communication channels open, remembering that *LOVE finds a way to COMMUNICATE, and it's his initiative* if he is going to love as CHRIST LOVED.

Metaphor

By contrast, a metaphor is not so straightforward. It communicates an impression more by implication. In the expressions, *"You are the salt of the earth . . ."* (Matt. 5:13) and *"You are the light of the world"* (Matt. 5:14), our Lord Jesus is multiplying metaphors to communicate graphic truth about the determinative role Christians are to play in affecting the world. In those early days, salt was the major means of arresting corruption in meat or fish, so the figure is not lost on those who listened to Jesus. Light, in any age, enables us to function with any degree of confidence. It dispels darkness. When we can't see, we're in trouble! The words "salt" and "light" are used as implied comparison. These metaphors speak with penetrating force, even though they are implicit in nature.

Irony

The use of irony as a figure of speech, though it has a bite to it, often has its humorous side. Our Lord was using both effects when he said, ". . . how can you say to your brother, 'Brother, let me take out the speck that is in your eye,' when you yourself do not see the log that is in your own eye?" (Luke 6:42).

In 1 Corinthians 4:8 the apostle Paul uses irony with great force, "Already you are filled! Already you have become rich! Without us you have become kings! And would that you did reign, so that we might share the rule with you." As we read on, Paul proceeds to contrast the state of the apostles as being the last—not the first, as spectacles to the world, as fools. Then he uses irony again, "We are fools for Christ's sake, but you are wise in Christ. We are weak, but you are strong. You are held in honor, but we in disrepute" (1 Cor. 4:10). Can you imagine how the Corinthian Christians must have felt the shame of their misplaced value systems, how this pointed word of sarcasm must have punctured their swollen pride in men? Would that we should review *our* value systems, today, and discover the only ground of boasting—the Lord Jesus and his life in us.

Metonymy

Then there's metonymy (a change of name). Speaking to the Pharisees concerning Herod, Christ says "Go and tell that *fox* . . ." (Luke 13:32) and with one word he characterized that politically crafty king. And, "The way of the fool is right in his own eyes . . ." (Prov. 12:15) where *eyes* represents the way he sees things, or his mental perspective. And, ". . . *the tongue* of the wise brings healing" (Prov. 12:18) in which *tongue* stands for what the wise one says, his words of wisdom.

In the New Testament, "Then went out to him Jerusalem and all Judea and all the region about the Jordan . . ." (Matt. 3:5) in which it is obvious that *people,* not places, are meant in the mention of these various regions. Then, we look at "You cannot drink the cup of the Lord and the cup of demons. You cannot partake of the table of the Lord and the table of demons" (1 Cor. 10:21). Here *cup* and *table* are used for what they contain and what they offer. Again, in Romans 3:30 *the circumcision* is used to represent the Jewish people, while *uncircumcision* refers to the Gentiles.

I'm sure from these examples you can see how commonly metonymy is used in the Bible. We use the same figure today when we call a person "a tiger" or "a kitten."

Hyperbole

Painting a picture larger than life by intentional exaggeration beyond reality is a common feature of our own speech, so hyperbole (*a throwing beyond*) should be thoroughly familiar to us.

In the anguish of his torment Job indulges in this kind of language. More graphically than any other form of speech it expresses the awfulness of his feeling of affliction.

And now my soul is poured out
    within me;
  days of affliction have taken hold
    of me.
The night racks my bones,
  and the pain that gnaws me takes
    no rest.
With violence it seizes my garment;
  it binds me about like the collar of
    my tunic.
God has cast me into the mire,
  and I have become like dust and
    ashes.
I cry to thee and thou dost not an-
    swer me;
  I stand, and thou dost not heed me.
Thou hast turned cruel to me;
  with the might of thy hand thou
    dost persecute me.
Thou liftest me up on the wind,
    thou makest me ride on it,
  and thou tossest me about in the
    roar of the storm.
Yea, I know that thou wilt bring me
    to death,
  and to the house appointed for all
    living (Job 30:16–23).

Certainly we get the keen sense of his utter despair from this highly expressive, but extravagant, language.

The apostle John in the New Testament uses hyperbolic language in this statement: "But there are also many other things which Jesus did; were every one of them to be written, I suppose that the world itself could not contain the books that would be written" (John 21:25). If we considered Christ's eternal existence, perhaps this statement could be taken literally, but if we limit it to the deeds of the Lord Jesus in his humanity (which I believe is what John has in mind) then it is clearly a use of hyperbole.

Personification

Referring to inanimate objects as if they possessed life and personality is especially evident in the language of imagination and feeling. In Numbers 16:32, ". . . the earth opened its mouth and swallowed them up . . ." speaks of Korah and his men. Here the earth is personified as having a mouth to devour these men.

The Lord Jesus uses personification in, "O Jerusalem, Jerusalem, killing the prophets and stoning those who are sent to you! How often would I have gathered your children together as a hen gathers her brood under her wings, and you would not!" (Matt. 23:37). The city of Jerusalem is here personified. Our Lord's concern was for its people, yet he addresses the city as if it were they.

Again, our Lord personifies *tomorrow* in these words: "Therefore do not be anxious about tomorrow, for tomorrow will be anxious for itself" (Matt. 6:34). Here *tomorrow* is invested with characteristics of human personality, as being beset with anxious cares.

Apostrophe

This is a strange but graphic figure which sounds as if the speaker were talking to himself in a sort of externalized soliloquy. For instance, David says to his dead son, "O my son Absalom, my son, my son Absalom! Would I had died instead of you, O Absalom, my son, my son!" (2 Sam. 18:33). What a moving expression of David's grief this is; no other mode of expression could be quite so expressive in this instance.

Then there is the use of this figure in which the kings of

earth address a fallen city, "Alas! alas! thou great city, thou mighty city, Babylon! In one hour has thy judgment come!" (Rev. 18:10).

This figure of speech seems best adapted to the expression of deep emotion. As such, it readily grabs our attention and draws out our interest.

Synechdoche

Here's one most of us never heard of, but which we frequently use in everyday speech. We say, "This is his hour" when we don't really mean an hour just sixty minutes long. We mean this is his time of glory, or suffering, or whatever we associate with his current experience. We have substituted a part for the whole. In scripture it occurs in such passages as this: in Judges 12:7 we are told Jephthah was buried "in the cities of Gilead" (Hebrew) though actually only one of those cities is meant; in Luke 2:1 "all the world" is used to mean the world of the Roman Empire; in Deuteronomy 32:41 "if I whet the lightning of my sword" the word *lightning* is used for the flashing edge of the gleaming blade.

Perhaps now we have seen enough of the prevalence and expressive value of figures of speech to help us appreciate the color and realism they lend to the language of the Bible. Also, interpretively, our review should take some of the mystery out of our encounters with these forms, in studying the Bible.

□ 8 □

The Language of Analogy

If we seriously examine the speech forms used in scripture we see that our Lord Jesus in his earthly ministry, as well as the writers of the New Testament books, all used various forms of the language of analogy. These are the communication modes which use comparison, resemblance, or correspondence (whichever term best expresses it) to lead us from familiar ground to new, unexplored realms of thought.

Analogy is "similarity in some respects between things otherwise unlike, a partial resemblance." Use of the language of analogy is seen in *parables, allegories,* and *types,* all of which employ this feature of resemblance, or correspondence. To my mind these represent the ultimate in pedagogy on God's part. In them he reveals truth in concealed forms, thus intriguing the human mind. He knows we all love a mystery, so he couches his truth in enigmatic terms. By this he also separates those who are merely toying with ideas from those others who are determined to pursue the clues to ultimate understanding of truth. Because of the very nature of these expressive literary forms, their interpretation is correspondingly more difficult and intensely challenging.

The word *parable* is from *para* (alongside) plus *bole* (throw), or, "to throw alongside." As we observe our Lord's use of this figure, we see that it is spiritual truth concealed in a story—the two being laid side-by-side.

Allegory is from *allos* (another, of the same kind) and *agoreuo,* "to speak" (originally in the Greek *agora,* the marketplace), thus, a story told in the marketplace. The dictionary says it is "a story in which the people and happenings have a symbolic meaning used for explaining or teaching ideas or moral principles."

Type is a term borrowed directly from the Greek *tupos* (the mark left by a blow, thus, imprint). We get our word *typical* from it, also *typeface* and *typewriter.* The dictionary says a type is "a model, a symbol, a person or thing that represents or symbolizes another, especially another that it is thought will appear later." Here are these three figures in chart form, phrased a bit differently.

Parable	A story which is true to reality and teaches a moral or spiritual lesson.
Allegory	A story in which people or things have hidden or symbolic meaning.
Type	A *real* parable, the details of which are woven by God into the *facts of history.*

While I have attempted to give general definitions to these forms of expression, if we view their usage in the Bible we find that they seem to defy exact and specific classification but rather blend into each other. I would suggest that they are so normal to the expression of thought that they are not meant to be rigidly categorized. They so flow out of the normal analogies of life's realities that God has chosen to use them as normative for the expression of truth. It would appear that the Bible is not concerned to make exact, sharp distinctions between these various forms.

In his *Notes on the Miracles and Parables of Our Lord,* Trench comments on parable as compared to allegory: "It remains to consider wherein parable differs from allegory. This it does in form rather than in essence; in the allegory an interpenetration of the thing signifying and the thing signified finding place, the qualities and properties of the first being attributed to the last, and the two thus blended together, instead of being kept quite distinct and placed side by side, as in the case of the parable." [1]

As I understand this statement, Trench is saying that the parable is a more direct side-by-side comparison, while the allegory is more an interweaving of parallel features blending together in the implied force of the words used. In other words, an allegory, with its implied comparisons is related to a parable, with its more formal, identifiable comparison just as a metaphor (an implied comparison) is related to a simile (a formal comparison). Add to this that a type combines the features of metaphor (as an implied comparison) with parable (a realistic story with a moral or spiritual lesson), the whole being implanted by God in historical fact. In this case, history is designed by God to teach a spiritual truth, and usually takes the form of Old Testament history as having an identifiable counterpart in the New Testament teaching of spiritual truth.

To illustrate: the Lord Jesus himself says to Nicodemus, ". . . as Moses lifted up the serpent in the wilderness, so must the Son of man be lifted up, that whoever believes in him may have eternal life" (John 3:15). Here our Lord clearly referring to the incident in Israel's history recorded in Numbers 21:9, "And the Lord said to Moses, 'Make a fiery serpent and set it on a pole; and every one who is bitten when he sees it shall live.' So Moses made a bronze serpent, and set

---

[1] R. E. Trench, *Notes on the Parables and Miracles of Our Lord* ('Old Tappan, N.J.: Fleming H. Revell Co., n.d.), p. 8.

it on a pole; and if a serpent bit any man, he would look at the bronze serpent and live" (Num. 21:8, 9).

Here is what I would call a type. Call it just an illustration if you will—whatever we call it, the important thing is to see the truth it is designed to convey. Clearly God ordered the event in Israel's history so that the Lord Jesus was prefigured in becoming God's remedy for sin. The coinciding features are too evident to be denied:

In The Old Testament Story	In New Testament Truths
Sin was the problem (Num. 21:5).	Sin is still the problem (John 3:19, 20).
Serpent originated and personifies sin (Gen. 3).	That old serpent, Satan, still brings sin and death (Rev. 20:2).
God sent serpents (picturing sin) to bring death (Num. 21:6).	Sin still brings death (Rom. 6:23).
God provided the antidote and remedy for sin and death (Num. 21:8,9).	God provided the remedy for sin and death. As the serpent was lifted up—so the Son of man (John 3:15). God so loved that he gave (John 3:16).
Serpent lifted up on a pole (Num. 21:8).	Christ was lifted up on a cross (John 19:17, 18).
The result: the one who looked at the bronze serpent lived (Num. 21:9).	The result: whoever believes in him should not perish but have eternal life (John 3:16).
The Lesson LIFE IN A LOOK BY FAITH	*The Lesson* LIFE IN A LOOK BY FAITH

I'm sure you have noticed that all of these figures, whether parable, allegory or type, are biblical terms right out of the Greek vocabulary of the New Testament. On that basis, if none other, we should seriously seek to gain what we can learn from these God-given expressions of truth. I hope you noticed, too, that all these words by their very definition express some form of correspondence, that is, the idea of laying one thing alongside another for the purpose of gaining additional understanding.

Now that we have this descriptive data, let's look at each of these modes of expression in more detail.

Parables

In a parable, the lesson is always woven into a story which is true to reality. There appears to be a time in our Lord's ministry when he shifted from the simple straightforward declaration of truth to the more veiled speech in parables. The transition is highlighted in Matthew 13:10–17, where his disciples, noting the change, asked him why he was speaking now in parables. Our Lord Jesus says, "This is why I speak to them in parables, because seeing they do not see, and hearing they do not hear, nor do they understand" (Matt. 13:13). Then he adds a quotation from Isaiah, ". . . this people's heart has grown dull, and their ears are heavy of hearing, and their eyes they have closed, lest they should perceive . . . and hear . . . and understand . . . and turn for me to heal them" (Matt. 13:14, 15).

In our day we would say, "There's no way he can confuse them with the facts—they've already made up their minds." So parables were, and are, designed to reveal the truth to those who really want to know it (as we see in the further questioning they aroused in the disciples), and to conceal the truth from men of casual curiosity or immovable commitment to their preconceived errors, such as we see in the Pharisees. Their having heard the truth, thus presented, becomes a judgment on their intransigence.

And though Christ's disciples were obviously puzzled at the time, it is certain that later events, in particular the death and resurrection of our Lord, must have unveiled much truth that had been stored in their memories through his parables. The same applies to the Pharisees. After his resurrection they must have spent some sleepless nights thinking of what Christ had said.

Fortunately, the Lord Jesus interprets some of his parables. This gives us a handle on our interpretive approach to them. The first one he interprets is "the parable of the sower" in Matthew 13:3–9. The explanation is in Matthew 13:18–23, in which Jesus identifies some of the pieces of the puzzle. Please follow it through in your own Bible.

The seed = the word of the kingdom

The birds = the evil one, the devil, who snatches away what is sown.

The soils = various heart responses to the Word.

    (1) *the path* = hardened ground where the seed never takes root and is eaten by birds, thus hardened hearts.

    (2) *rocky ground* = the shallow commitment which does not endure under stress.

    (3) *the thorny ground* = the heart so preoccupied with worldly, material things that it allows them to choke out the seed of the Word.

        (a) the thorns are worldly cares and riches.

    (4) *the fruitful soil* = the heart that hears the Word with understanding, and responds.

It is clear that our Lord intends a definite correspondence of figure with reality, and from the immediate context it is clear that the issue focuses on the unbelief of the Jews as a pointed lesson to his disciples (and us). Essentially, he is saying, "Where is your heart?"

The next parable he interprets follows in this same chapter (Matt. 13:24–30) which Jesus' disciples call "the parable of the weeds of the field" (v. 36).

Again our Lord identifies the figures (Matt. 13:36–43):

The sower = the Son of man (Jesus himself)

The field = the world

The seed (now different) = the sons of the kingdom–now not the Word, but believers

The weeds = the sons of the evil one

The weed sower = the devil

The harvest = the close of the age (not before)

The reapers = the angels

Once again, the central point is clear. Christ's men are to allow the true and the false to exist side-by-side and let the sower (Christ) do the sorting out at the end of the age. Jesus is giving a preview of his role as judge and pointing up the seriousness of men's response to him and to his word. The prospect is either weeping and gnashing of teeth—or shining like the sun, in righteousness.

From here on it gets more difficult to interpret our Lord's parables, for he puts us on our own. However, we can formulate a few guidelines from these illustrations:

(1) We can expect to see a correlation of the physical features of the parable to the spiritual implications involved.

(2) The point of the parable is designed to speak to the situation at hand, observable by the context, thus we should seek to gain one solid point of application to the problem evident in the hearers, as we relate parable to context.

(3) Our Lord revealed the hidden meaning to believing hearts then; he will do so for us now, if we seek enlightenment from him as did these early disciples.

(4) If we have understood what seems to be the central teaching of the parable, let's apply *that* truth, and not strain to make all the details fit some esoteric personal slant.

Parables about Lost Things

Now, let's try our hand at a parable the Lord has *not* interpreted for us. As a matter of fact, let's tackle *three* of them in Luke 15. Our Lord joins these together: the lost sheep, the lost coin, and the lost sons. So we see that these three comprise one subject, a parable about lost things.

I am not going to reproduce the text here, but I assume that you will read it from your own Bible, as if we were studying together. And as I read "the parable of the lost sheep" I note first it is set against the complaint of the Pharisees about the fact that "Jesus receives sinners and eats with them."

To this the Lord Jesus replies with these parables. The lost sheep story (Luke 15:3–7) highlights the value of the sheep to its owner and the joy he expresses at its recovery. The application of the story makes it clear that the Lord Jesus is the shepherd of the sheep, and his concern is to seek the lost ones. "Just so, I tell you, there will be more joy in heaven over one sinner who repents than over ninety-nine righteous persons who need no repentance" (Luke 15:7). This punch line must have hit hard at the self-righteous Pharisees who didn't lift a finger to help lost sinners—only criticized the one who did. But even stronger than this is the revelation of God's attitude toward sinners, and the obvious value he puts on each of us— so much that heaven rejoices when one lost one is rescued by the Savior.

The Lost Coin . . .

The next one, the lost coin, needs a bit of Hebrew cultural background. The ten coins were probably part of the woman's marriage dowry. As Fred H. Wight points out:

> Since a divorced wife in the Orient is entitled to all her wearing apparel, for this reason much of her personal dowry consists of coins on her headgear, or jewelry on her person. This becomes wealth to her in case her marriage ends in failure. This is why the dowry is so important to the bride, and such emphasis is placed upon it in the negotiations that precede marriage. The woman who had ten pieces of silver and lost one was greatly concerned over her loss, because it was doubtless part of her marriage dowry.[2]

So we start by recognizing that the coin in some measure represented this woman's security, since in her Oriental culture

---

[2] Fred H. Wight, *Manners and Customs in Bible Lands* (Chicago: Moody Press, n.d.) p. 128.

she was practically defenseless against divorce for any capricious reason. In losing the coin, she lost some of her security.

In application, our Lord says, "Just so, I tell you, there is joy before the angels of God over one sinner who repents" (Luke 15:10). The joy is the same in heaven, but the added element of restored *security* (for one who was distraught) is the cause of rejoicing.

The Lost Sons . . .

Looking at the third parable in this trio, the lost sons, we discover another addition. (This parable is usually called "the parable of the prodigal son," but if we look carefully there were two sons, each lost in his own way.) The issue here is *enjoyment,* for the wandering son had sought pleasure, only to forfeit the joy of his father's house, while the stay-at-home son had apparently never known the joy that was there with the father, being filled with self-centered, legalistic resentment (I see this from his statement in verses 28–30).

The closing scene is one of enjoyment—love, fellowship, music, being expressed in a merry party. The key figure here is the father, who is clearly representative of the heavenly Father. The better title for the story is "The Waiting Father," for the yearning heart of God filled with concern for his lost ones is beautifully expressed in the narrative. We don't know whether the older son ever joined the party. He could have done so at any time, but the Lord Jesus, as the master storyteller, leaves this an open question.

Can you see how these three stories were designed to hit the Pharisees right where they lived? They portray the heart attitude of God toward lost ones. He desires for each of us *safety* in his fold, *security* against all that threatens our peace of mind, and *enjoyment* of all the good things of a loving Father's house. His program is all profit, no loss, for his people. I'm sure there is much more we could gain from these beautifully expressive stories, but we have seen, I trust, that it is possible for us to understand parables.

To add to my own personal observations of parables, I worked through a basic textbook on the subject, Trench, *Notes on the Miracles and the Parables of Our Lord,* seeking to condense and summarize his conclusions on this subject. Here is what I learned:

Why Jesus Taught in Parables

Our Lord used parables to teach spiritual truth through well-known physical counterparts. Parables are not just happily-chosen illustrations from a library of storybooks; they have their ground in the nature of reality. The corresponding images belong to each other, as Trench says, "by an inward necessity; they were linked together long before by the law of secret affinity . . . ."

> It is not merely that these analogies assist to make the truth intelligible . . . their power lies deeper than this, in the harmony unconsciously felt by all men . . . between the natural and spiritual worlds, so that analogies from the first are felt to be something more than illustrations. They are arguments, and may be alleged as witnesses; the world of nature being throughout a witness for the world of spirit, proceeding from the same hand, growing out of the same root, and being constituted for that very end.[3]

Parables employ a visible world to lead us to understand the invisible things of God. Here God communicates in terms of human relationships and natural phenomena—the ordinary stuff of which life is made. Again quoting Trench:

> . . . besides his revelation in words, God has another and an older, and one indeed without which it is inconceivable how that

---

[3] R. E. Trench, *Notes on the Miracles and Parables of Our Lord* (Old Tappan, N.J.: Revell Publishing Co., n.d.) pp. 12 & 13 on parables.

other could be made, for from this it appropriates all its signs of communication. This entire moral and visible world from first to last, with its kings and its subjects, its parents and its children, its sun and its moon, its sowing and its harvest, its light and its darkness, its sleeping and its waking, its birth and its death, is from beginning to end a mighty parable, a great teaching of supersensuous truth, a help at once to our faith and to our understanding.[4]

Even the fallenness of God's creation sounds forth its clear but unhappy truth about the imperfection of the present order; poisonous reptiles, natural catastrophes, diseased and deteriorating bodies, poison oak and gadflies—all testify of the fact and results of man's fall. And all point to the need for a better order of things.

In parables, Christ moves our thought processes from familiar ground to new concepts, from the known to the unknown, from the physical to the spiritual. In parables he appeals not just to the intelligent reason of man, but to his imagination and to his feelings. They have all the appeal of a human interest story. Truth imparted in this form has a lingering quality not always true of more abstract modes of expression. To quote Trench again:

His words, laid up in the memory, were to many that heard Him like the money of another country, unavailable for present use, —the value of which they only dimly knew, but which yet was ready in their hand, when they reached that land, and were naturalized in it. And thus must it ever be with all true knowledge, which is not the communication of information, the transfer of a dead sum of capital of facts or theories from one mind to another, but the opening of living fountains within the heart. . . .[5]

---

[4] Ibid., pp. 16 and 19 on parables.
[5] Ibid., p. 26 on parables.

Rules for Interpreting Parables

The values of parabolic teachings seem evident, but we need help in understanding them. How do we get out of them the truth the Lord intends to teach? Here are some suggestions:

1. *Seek to understand the one central truth the parable teaches,* as distinguished from the corollary truths or facts which relate to it.

2. *Relate all the peripheral details to this central truth,* seeking to grasp how they contribute to the central truth to make it shine more clearly.

3. *Relate the parable to the context which introduces it and that which follows.* Here we often find the key to its meaning—in seeing how the parable applies to the situation at hand. Again, Trench has a pertinent word on this subject:

> These helps to interpretation, (that is, the clues derived from the context) though rarely or never lacking, are yet given in no fixed or formal manner; sometimes they are supplied by the Lord Himself (Matt. 22:14; 25:13); sometimes by the inspired narrators of his words (Luke 15:2, 3; 18:9; 19:11); sometimes, as the epilogue, they follow (Matt. 24:13; Luke 16:9). Occasionally a parable is furnished with these helps to a right understanding both at its opening and its close; as is that of the Unmerciful Servant (Matt. 18:23), which is suggested by the question which Peter asks (ver. 21), and wound up by the application which the Lord Himself makes (ver. 35). So again the parable at Matt. 20:1–15 begins and finishes with the same saying, and Luke 12:16–20 is supplied with the same amount of help for its right understanding.[6]

4. *A parable should not be the primary, much less exclusive, foundation for any doctrine.* Do not use parables to establish a doctrinal base; establish your doctrinal foundations from

---

[6] Ibid., p. 39 on parables.

the clear teaching of scripture elsewhere, then parables will serve to illustrate and confirm, adding light and color to truth already discovered.

5. *Avoid strained interpretations.* If you have to work hard at justifying your interpretive opinion, it's probably not worth contending for. A correct interpretation is not easy to arrive at, but having been discovered, should be easy to live with. It should have a sense of fitness.

6. *Extremes of interpretation should be avoided.* One extreme is to seek only the most general, limited significance, the other is to make every minute detail say something.

7. *Hard-and-fast, absolute rules for interpreting parables have not been given to us.* The best we can do is to observe the way our Lord interpreted the parables in Matthew 13 and seek to learn from him. *Much that we gain from parables will be determined by our own reverent approach to Scripture as God's Word, our total grasp of biblical truth, and our spiritually-minded common sense.*

□ 9 □

Allegories and Types

A considerably advanced degree of interpretive skill is needed for unraveling the truth woven into *allegories* and *types*. But note that in every case there are known quantities which by comparison and correspondence are designed to lead us to an understandable interpretation. It is not surprising that there are extremes of interpretive opinion regarding these forms, as the interpreter's task is an imposing one. On the one hand we view with alarm the excesses of some of the early church fathers, who took such leaps of interpretive fancy that the whole idea of types and allegories has been discredited, or at least discounted, by some modern Bible scholars as what they call "allegorizing" or "spiritualizing" the text. On the other hand, since these figures are identifiable in the Bible itself when it uses the term "type" or "allegory," we do well not to throw out that which God has apparently determined to use. He is so much more imaginative than we are! So, being willing to face the difficulties, let's give God a chance to enlighten us with the communication tools he has devised.

Allegories

The one allegory in the Bible that is so labeled is in Galatians 4:21–2: "Now this is an allegory" Paul says in verse 24.

So we have at least one identifiable example of this figure of speech. Paul writes,

> Tell me, you who desire to be under law, do you not hear the law? For it is written that Abraham had two sons, one by a slave and one by a free woman. But the son of the slave was born according to the flesh, the son of the free woman through promise. *Now this is an allegory:* these women are two covenants. One is from Mount Sinai, bearing children for slavery; she is Hagar. Now Hagar is Mount Sinai in Arabia; she corresponds to the present Jerusalem, for she is in slavery with her children. But Jerusalem above is free, and she is our mother (Gal. 4:21–26, italics mine).

At first look, our task seems rather formidable, but let's try to sort out the pieces that correspond. I suggest the key is, "*. . . these women are two covenants.*" So I proceed to try to sort out the various references under these headings.

I read the context in the book of Galatians, also the Old Testament account to which Paul is referring (Gen. 16:1–18:15 and 21:1–21), so that I'll have the whole story in mind, and here's what I see as a result:

Two Covenants

Hagar	Sarah
Old Covenant—The *Law of Moses*	*New Covenant*—The *Promised Spirit*
Mt. Sinai—Law	*Mt. Moriah—Grace*
Jerusalem—The *Present Earthly One*	*Jerusalem*—The *One Above*, the *Heavenly One*
Slavery	**Freedom**
The Flesh i.e. human effort, human ideas, worldly thought patterns	*The Promise*—to be *Believed* i.e. counting on what God has said

We can see even more if we use another key phrase, *"Now we, brethren, like Isaac, are children of promise"* (Gal 4: 28). This suggests another comparison.

Two Kinds of Children

Ishmael Son of a Slave	Isaac Son of a Free Woman
In *Slavery* with his *Mother*	*Free* like his *Mother*
Child of the *Flesh*	*Child* of *Promise*
Persecutor of the one *Born* of the *Spirit*	*Persecuted* by the one *Born* of the *Flesh*
Cast out, with his *mother*— no inheritance	Has an *inheritance, freedom in Christ* "For freedom Christ has set us free; stand fast therefore, and do not submit again to the yoke of slavery" (Gal. 5:1).

"We" Christians, says Paul, *"are like Isaac!"* And, by implication at least, *not* like Ishmael.

And when you reflect that in Galatians Paul is addressing Gentile Christians, it seems as if he expected a great deal from them, interpretively. How could they grasp such a far-out figure? Well, it's not hard to envision when we remember he was countering the arguments of the Judaizers, who had taught these Galatians that the works of the law were necessary, for salvation and for sanctification. Where but to the Old Testament (from which these false teachers quoted) would Paul go to expose their fallacies?

What interpretive principles can we draw from this biblical example of allegory? Here's what I see:

1. Allegory is a bona-fide figure of speech used in the Bible.

2. It employs comparison and correspondence of words and ideas.

3. It is illustrative and explanatory of a specific line of truth.

4. It cannot be divorced from its local context or the historical narrative from which it is drawn.

5. It is comprised of a number of metaphorical expressions in which the meaning of one word is invested in another, e.g. Hagar is Mt. Sinai, that is, she represents the Law of Moses.

6. None of the figurative expressions are so obscure as to leave us guessing as to their import.

7. We can expect to learn something from their use that will be of profit—applicable to life.

8. We would be wise not to assume that such hidden meanings are latent in every place in the Bible.

Are there other legitimate uses of allegory in the Bible, even though not specifically identified as such? I don't know. This is the only one specifically identified in the Bible. What is important, and what I do know, is that God wants us to recognize that here he has established a valid vehicle of communication using the idea of word correspondence, in which one word can represent all the implications of a broad concept (Hagar = Mt. Sinai = the Law).

Certainly we see the same sort of thing, though not so elaborately spelled out, in "For *Christ our Passover* also has been sacrificed" (1 Cor. 5:7 NASV, italics mine). Here the mind turns immediately to the question, in what ways does the Passover picture the Lord Jesus in his sacrifice? So we turn back to Exodus 12 where the Passover was instituted by God and proceed to think it through. I would commend it to you as a most enlightening exercise of your interpretive skill.

The same feature of correspondence is true of ". . . all drank the same spiritual drink, for they were drinking from a spiritual rock which followed them; and *the rock was Christ*"

(1 Cor. 10:4 NASV). Again our minds are drawn back to Israel's wilderness journey to investigate what God had in mind for us to learn through this mind-intriguing method of teaching. Whether we call these allegories or not is unimportant as long as we discover their hidden truths. However, I'm inclined to think there are more allegories hidden in the Bible than we give God credit for. Stuart Briscoe, in his delightful and careful treatise on Ezekiel,[1] is not ashamed to say so. He calls Ezekiel's bizarre acting-out of the "Word of the Lord" allegorical. In trying to interpret this difficult book, one is inclined to agree.

Types

It is exceedingly unfortunate that modern scholarship has succeeded in almost eliminating the investigation and teaching of typology as a valid interpretive pursuit. So much has been lost of the richness and practical illustrative value which I believe God intends we should have through an understanding of types. I would like to try to regain something of this lost value, using the Bible itself as the foundation for its validity.

Typology is a bad word in many theological circles, but it is not difficult to see that God has a use for it, even if we do not. It is easy to see why many have reacted adversely to this field of biblical interpretation, for one only needs to read some of the writings of the past centuries to see the tendency to overreach in this obviously fascinating use of figurative language.

Much of the problem would be resolved, however, by simply agreeing on what a *type* is. The definition can be broad or narrow, based on the source of information we employ. I would remind you once again, the word *type* is borrowed from the Greek *tupos,* which is a mark formed by a blow or impression, hence a figure or image. Right now you are reading the

---

[1] Stuart Briscoe, *All Things Weird and Wonderful* (Wheaton: Victor Books, 1977), p. 118.

mark made by *type*face, each letter, word and paragraph conveying by the use of agreed-upon symbols the thoughts which have been set in "type." We use the word *typical,* meaning that which bears the impress of some distinctive pattern of design, thought, and so on. So if we want to draw our definition of a biblical *type* from this basic data, then we can see widespread use of types in the Bible such as one can read in Wilson's *Dictionary of Bible Types.*

Dr. Walter Wilson's "types" range from items like:

YOKE
Gen. 27:40 (b) This type is used to indicate the oppression and repression placed upon one person by another person, or upon one nation by another nation.

Matt. 11:29 (b) This term is used to indicate the blessed union for service which the Lord desires on the part of His people. The Christian, walking with the Lord and serving Him, finds the work to be easy, and the load is light.

2 Cor. 6:14 (b) In this case the yoke represents an unhappy union of those who are saved with those who are unsaved in any service or work. The Lord commands His people to be linked up only with Christians, and not with those who belong to Satan's family. This refers to marriage, to business, and to every other form of union. This situation is complicated frequently by those who are saved, born again, after the union is made. God made provision for this situation in various parts of His Word.[2]

to his entry on:

SCAPEGOAT
Lev. 16:8 (b) The goats in this story represent two aspects of the sacrifice of the Lord Jesus. The live goat which became the scapegoat is a picture of the Savior living in glory with the marks of Calvary upon Him, having taken away the sin of the world, and having died at Calvary for our sins. The dead goat represents Christ at Calvary, giving up His life for us.[3]

---

[2] Walter L. Wilson, *Dictionary of Bible Types* (Grand Rapids: William B. Eerdmans Co., 1957), p. 519.
[3] Ibid., p. 396.

Certainly these are figurative words containing the feature of correspondence to which we have alluded, but they differ widely in their usage. The word *yoke* has general usage as implying "two joined together in a working union," while the word *scapegoat* has a specific identification with the sacrifices ordered under the Levitical priesthood. To make any sense at all, this latter word must be viewed in the tight context of Leviticus 16. I question whether *yoke* should be called a type; however, *scapegoat* comes much closer to the biblical significance of that term, in my estimation.

We can draw the lines a bit tighter if we say a *type* is a person or thing prefiguring a future person or thing; or a figure or example of something future and more or less prophetic called the antitype. Then we can define the antitype as: a thing formed after some pattern, or a thing resembling another, its counterpart—or something which answers to a type. Essentially, I see a type as a figurative expression picturing, in shadow form, an identifiable reality elsewhere presented in scripture. Both *type* and *antitype* are New Testament biblical terms, as we shall illustrate later.

My own composite expression of all I have grasped on the subject is this: I see a type as being *a premeditated resemblance which God has built into the Bible and history to illustrate and teach truth—to make it easier to grasp than if it were only stated in prosaic and propositional terms.* It is a kindness of God to stir our minds and imagination by the use of types —to make an unforgettable impress. I see it as God's way of "putting his brand on our brain" so that we cannot escape the impact of truth.

Under the general heading of typology, then, we could group various terms, all derived from scripture, portraying slightly different forms of this figure. I would like to list these and illustrate each one (see chart on the next page).

Typology

FIGURE	MEANING	EXAMPLE
TYPE Gk. *tupos*	A planned correspondence between two biblical accounts designed by God to teach and illustrate truth.	1 Cor. 10:6&11 Israel (the nation) a type of the individual Christian
ANTITYPE Gk. *antitupon*	A thing resembling another, its counterpart.	Heb. 9:24 High priest in tabernacle the figure; Christ appearing before God on our behalf, the reality.
PATTERN Gk. *hupotuposis*	A pattern placed before one to be held fast and copied.	1 Tim. 1:16 Paul, a pattern, as the object of God's grace and mercy.
EXAMPLE Gk. *hupodeigma*	A representation or copy. From verb: *to show by placing under*, as a template to be followed and copied.	John 13:15 Christ—the example of a truly "servant" heart.
SHADOW Gk. *skia*	An image cast by an object and representing the form of that object —but not its substance or reality.	Heb. 8:5 The tabernacle, an earthly shadow of the heavenly realities.
SIGN Gk. *semeion*	A distinctive mark or feature which is used to identify and/or reveal the character of a person or thing.	2 Cor. 12:12 That which marks out a true apostle.

Perhaps it would be helpful to identify the use of some of these words in the New Testament to see their use in context:

1. *Tupos*

> John 20:25—*print* (or mark) of the nails
> Acts 7:43—*figures* (idol images) of foreign gods
> Acts 23:25—a letter of this *type* (following this pattern) or "to this effect"
> Romans 5:14—Adam, a *type* (or pattern) of Christ
> Romans 6:17—a *type* (or standard) of teaching
> 1 Cor. 10:6—these things (Israel's history, the rock picturing Christ, etc.) are *types.*
> 1 Cor. 10:11—now these things happened to them *typically,* for our admonition.
> Phil. 3:17—you have us as a *type* (or pattern)
> 1 Thess. 1:7—so you became a *type* (or pattern) to all that believe.
> 1 Tim. 4:12—but you became a *type* (or pattern) of the believers, in speech and behavior.
> Tit. 2:7—in all things showing yourself a *pattern* of good works.
> Heb. 8:5—make all things according to the *pattern* shown to you in the mount
> 1 Pet. 5:3—becoming *examples* to the flock

Here we see all the uses of *tupos* in the Greek New Testament and can identify the various meanings given to this word, all relating to its basic import, but some becoming a much more extensive and formal usage, as we can determine by setting them in their context.

For instance, the "print" (*tupos*) of the nails in the hands of Jesus obviously carries the basic sense of "a mark made by striking a blow," and we do not look for any deeper meaning than this. On the other hand, when we see that "Adam . . . was a type of the one who was to come" (i.e. Christ) we are immediately alerted to seek the answer to the question, "In what way?" Certainly he was not a type in reference to sin, since Adam began the pattern of disobedience we have all perpetuated, while the Lord Jesus never sinned. So as we read the whole of Romans 5, we have a study in comparisons and contrasts in which we see that the way Adam typified Christ is that each was the source and beginning of a far-reaching fallout of consequences that have affected the whole of mankind. Here is the resemblance—and the theological implications are terrific! A clear understanding of this comparison in Romans 5 is a wide-open window toward understanding God and man.

Then there's the clearly specified typology of the resemblance (whether by comparison or contrast) of the Old Testament priesthood of Aaron and of Melchizedek with the high-priestly ministry of the Lord Jesus. In Hebrews 8:5 we have three of the words in our chart :

"They (the Old Testament tabernacle and priesthood) serve a *copy* (*hupodeigma*) and *shadow* (*skia*) of the heavenly sanctuary; for when Moses was about to erect the tent he was instructed by God, saying, 'See that you make everything according to the *pattern* (*tupos*) which was shown you in the mountain.' "

Certainly here is the clear declaration of God's intent to implant deeply significant truth in the worship and form of the tabernacle, investing deep levels of truth in the physical forms and actions to impart spiritual understanding. Evidently God gave Moses a *blueprint*—not just of form and furniture, but of the shadows and examples woven into his pattern, pointing to the realities which they picture. Our understanding of the Book of Hebrews revolves around our tracing through these analogies.

But the anchor point for our basic approach to the study of types rests in 1 Corinthians 10.

Now these things are *types* of us, so that we might not be

craving after evil things as indeed those were craving (1 Cor. 10:6, literal rendering, italics mine)

And again:

> . . . These things happened to those men *typically* and were written down for admonition of us upon whom the ends of the ages have come down (1 Cor. 10:11, literal rendering, italics mine).

Here is a wide-open door of typical teaching, for Israel is cited as an example, essentially a negative one, warning us against doing as they did. The target for the truth thus communicated is specifically designated as Christians in this later age, the church age. But how do we identify the point of analogy? Is each Israelite a type, or the nation? I have found that the key to a consistent application of this typology is to recognize that the *nation* Israel is picturing the *individual* Christian. When we keep that in mind the analogy fits and we can learn the lessons God has for us in this type.

Let's explore Israel's wilderness experience as an example to see if (1) we can match the *type with its antitype,* and (2) learn the needed lessons.

Hebrews 3:12, speaking of Israel's wilderness wanderings says: "Take care, brethren, lest there be in you an evil, unbelieving heart, leading you to fall away from the living God" (Heb. 3:12).

It seems we should learn an important lesson from Israel's experience—but *what* lesson?

Reviewing Israel's history, we start with her departure from Egypt (the beginning of redemption) and follow her story into the land of promise (the place of rest). Let's trace it through. In Exodus 12 and 13, beginning with the Passover, we see God's preparation for Israel's release from slavery; the Red Sea crossing and the wilderness journey is the trial of their faith; the entry and conquest of the land is entering into the victory and fulfillment of being in the place of God's appointment, despite obstacles.

Please read at least Exodus 3, 4, 12 and 13; Numbers 13 and 14; Deuteronomy 34; Joshua 1 through 8 to get the most out of this study. Then correlate with Hebrews 3 and 4 in the New Testament.

Release from Slavery

The beginning of freedom is *Christ—our Passover* (1 Cor. 5:7). This expression cites an obvious analogy, but what are the similarities? We discover them by reading Exodus 3 through 13 to get the background, observing especially chapter 12, as it relates to Christ our passover in 1 Corinthians 5:7, noting the resemblance features. Christ is the reality— the passover is the shadow.

♦ *A Lamb Slain*—a picture of redemption, setting free from bondage and death (John 1:29). Christ died for us.

♦ *Blood Sprinkled*—application and identification, the activity of faith (John 6:27–29).

♦ *The Lamb Eaten*—strength and sustenance for life (John 6:53).

♦ *Unleavened Bread*—strength for life's journey based on the putting away of sin and feeding on Christ. Corresponds to Christ the Bread of Life in John 6. (See also 1 Cor. 5:6–8)

♦ *Circumcision*—the mark of God's ownership, the judging of the principle of independent self-effort (cutting off the flesh) (Col. 2:9–11, Phil. 3:3).

♦ *Readiness to Travel*—a willingness to move out at God's command—out of bondage into the place of freedom and victory.

The Trial of Faith

♦ *The Dead Sea*—God's power to deliver through the tight spots. Also his cutting off the way back—no returning to the former bondage.

♦ *Israel*—(prince with God, or one who prevails with God) is a picture of the Christian believer.

♦ *Egypt*—bondage to Satan as god of this world, through the appeal of the world.

♦ *Dying in the Wilderness*—the result of unbelief—always death.

♦ *Manna*—God's sustaining grace even in the face of rebellion.

♦ *Jordan River*—the trial of faith: to repudiate the flesh and obey God despite circumstances and feelings (the flood condition). Corresponds to our experience of Romans 6—we died with Christ, thus freed from sin's power.

Entering God's Rest

♦ *Canaan*—the place of victory and rest in the midst of conflict.

♦ *Caleb*—the typical man of faith—conquering through God's power.

♦ *Jericho*—conquest and victory through faith in the certain Word of God. The foolishness of God is wiser than men (1 Cor. 1:25).

♦ *Ai*—(a heap of ruin) defeat through self-confidence and incomplete obedience.

♦ *Giants*—seemingly invincible, unconquerable obstacles.

♦ *Possessing the Land*—(only as the soles of their feet trod the ground) the walk of faith, taking possession of what is already ours—believing and acting on God's promises.

♦ *Moses*—not able to enter the land—the Law's inability to get us into the place of rest and victory.

♦ *Joshua*—a picture of Jesus (same word) as the trailblazer or pioneer of faith who is able to lead us into the place of victory and rest.

Our research has taken us through large portions of Exodus, Numbers, Deuteronomy, and Joshua in the Old Testament, while Hebrews 3 and 4 presents the New Testament application of the type. Here we see the imperative nature of a life of faith, of fully entering God's rest. By contrast, we can see in Numbers 13:17 to 14:35 the fatal consequences of unbelief. Through all this, Israel pictures in physical, historical terms the spiritual realities of the Christian life of a New Testament believer in Christ.

In application, we are here presented with clear testimony that we must believe God's Word and act on his promises if we are to enjoy a life of fulfillment and victory over the enemy forces. REST should be a most important word in the Christian vocabulary—and it is only experienced through the obedience of faith. "Therefore, while the promise of entering his rest remains [like *today*] let us fear lest any of you be judged to have failed to reach it. For good news came to us just as to them . . ." (Heb. 4:1, 2).

In this rather telling illustration we can discern something of the value of the study of types, for they have the capacity to make an indelible impression on the mind and heart in a uniquely helpful way. If you are yet unconvinced, I suggest you read the highly interesting treatment of the book of Esther by my fellow-pastor, Ray Stedman. His book is entitled *The Queen and I* (Word). The clincher, for me, on the typological nature of Esther is the Hebrew names of Haman's ten sons as Mr. Stedman points out in Chapter 10. Read it and see what you conclude, will you?

Some years ago I endeavored to pin down some principles for interpreting symbols and types, and as I review my conclusions, I feel they are still valid. Here are my suggestions. I hope you will find them helpful.

Biblical Symbols and Types

Rules for Interpretation

1. Look for the *basic* meaning of the symbol. Go beyond the superficial.
2. The *physical* is often used to picture the *spiritual*.
3. Look for the consistent use of a specific symbol in the Old Testament.
4. The symbol or type *must* be an illustration of and consistent with New Testament truth.
5. Recognize that the Old Testament teaches the same truth as the New Testament.
6. Don't expect the type to cover every subject of theology—limit to the topic under consideration in the context.
7. Assume that details given have meaning—seek to discover that meaning. However, don't expect *every* detail to fit. Every *analogy,* by its very nature, falls short of the full *reality*.
8. Identify *interpretational constants* by determining an accurate definition of any type or symbol which fits *all* the uses of that term in Scripture, e.g. "Lion" symbolizes power, whether applied to Satan as "a roaring lion" or to Christ as the "lion of the tribe of Judah."

Phase 3

Biblical Languages

10

The Greeks Had a Word for It

The Greek language is uniquely suited to the communication of God's truth, for it has modes of expression so concise and accurate in their descriptive power as to defy fullness of translation into English without becoming unwieldy. That's one reason we have so many New Testament translations, as scholars endeavor to carry over the full import of the Greek into English. So, the careful interpreter of the Bible does well to gain access to the meaning of the Greek which stands behind our English versions.

In addition, it is helpful to know that the New Testament came to us in what is called Koine, or "common" Greek. It is not the language of the classics or the poets, but the common, ordinary language of everyday popular usage. Modern archeology has done tremendous service to the New Testament student by unearthing and clarifying Greek terms that were otherwise obscure. In so doing, the archeologist's spade has buried the destructive critics of the New Testament record under the piles of evidence gleaned from pottery shard, parchment, and papyrus. It is encouraging to know that archeology has confirmed, not denied, the accuracy of our New Testament text, which was written in language the common people could grasp.

Historically, the conquests of Alexander the Great made Greek the language used throughout his broad empire, to the extent that it even carried over into the Roman world of New Testament times. God not only authored the Bible, I believe he providentially provided the language in which he planned to communicate his truth. This is especially true of the Greek of the New Testament, but also applies to the Hebrew of the Old Testament, of which we will have more to say later.

As I have previously stated, it is perfectly possible for the English reader to gain significant understanding of New Testament Greek without knowing Greek. This is because of the intense scholarship that has been applied in this field and expressed in English.

My introduction to this material was through the writings of Kenneth Wuest, now available in a three-volume edition of *Word Studies in the Greek New Testament for the English Reader.* And if you want to whet your appetite for more, read his sections on *Golden Nuggets from the Greek New Testament, Untranslatable Riches from the Greek New Testament,* and *Bypaths in the Greek New Testament.* Also, if you can get it, read his *Studies in the Vocabulary of the Greek New Testament.* These books will give you a look at some of the added insight on the New Testament available through even a minimal understanding of Greek. We have already mentioned the most basic tool for this purpose, Vine's *Expository Dictionary of New Testament Words.* Add to these Robertson's *Word Pictures in the New Testament* (in five volumes), and you will have a basic library on this subject. These helps are all designed for use by the English reader. Additional helps for the *Greek* reader are included in the Appendix.

Greek Thought Patterns

The most graphic and expressive word form in Greek is the verb. Here we find such a distinct difference from our English verb usage that we need to learn to think like a Greek. The function of verbs in any language is to express action; thus verb forms carry the greatest weight in the expression of thought. In English, our verbs emphasize the *time* of the action, so English verb tenses are the familiar past, present, and future, with their related forms. But Greek verbs emphasize *kind* of action, with time relationships being secondary. The Greek is more concerned with the manner in which the action takes place than the time at which it occurred, though he is not unmindful of time factors. So we need to change our normal thought pattern to accommodate this difference. With this in mind, let's examine Greek verb structure in more detail.

The major features of verbs, you may recall, are tense, mood, and voice.

♦ *Tense* expresses time and/or duration of action.
♦ *Mood* expresses the writer's or speaker's attitude toward the action.
♦ *Voice* expresses the action as either *performed* by the subject of the verb or *received* by the subject. The subject is either acting or being acted upon.

Let's look at these in chart form:

Greek Verb Tenses

TENSE	KIND OF ACTION	TIME
Present	*Continuous*, or *Durative*, like ⟶	*Present*
Aorist	*Viewed* as a *Whole*, without defining the manner of its occurrence	*Past* in the indicative mood only
Perfect	*Completed*, with ongoing results, like ⟶•⟶	Action completed in the past, with *present* continuing results
Imperfect	*Continuous*, like ⟶	*Past*
Future	*Undefined*, like the Aorist tense	*Future*

Present Tense

The Greek present tense, expressed in English terms reflects the idea *I am going* instead of *I go,* the action being in process.

Aorist Tense

The aorist tense (*aoristos,* the Greek word from which it comes, means undefined, indefinite, unhorizoned) is perhaps the most unusual from our standpoint. It is what I call the "splash" tense, for the Greek splashes it around in his speech when he is not trying to make any special distinctions such as the other tenses would convey. Dana and Mantey's *Manual Grammar of the Greek New Testament* tells us that the aorist signifies nothing as to manner of occurrence or completeness, it just makes reference to the action as happening. The aorist tense states the fact of the action without regard to its duration, viewing the event as a whole. It has been likened to a snapshot, whereas the present tense is like a moving picture.

There is the common misconception that the aorist tense specifies once-for-all action. It should be evident from the very name of the tense, aorist (undefined, indefinite) that this is not so. However, there are other factors in a particular context that would carry this meaning, such as the use of the Greek word *hapax,* meaning once, or once for all. In Hebrews 9:28, literally translated, we read ". . . so also Christ, having been offered once for all to bear the sins of many . . . ." We get the "once for all" idea from *hapax* and the context. "Having been offered" is in the aorist tense and contributes nothing to our understanding as to the duration or finality of the action. It considers the offering of Christ as an event, and is truly indefinite as to its manner of occurrence or completeness.

To illustrate the use of the present and aorist together, John 10:38b reads in literal rendering, ". . . in order that you may know (aorist tense) and be knowing (that is, continue to know, present tense) that the Father is in me and I in the Father." Here there is reference to the *fact* of knowing and the *continuing process* of knowing. Perhaps this is the best way to see the use of the aorist, by contrasting it with the use of the present tense in the same context. Dana and Mantey [1] give a telling illustration of this contrast:

> On the question of the believer's relation to sin, it is exceedingly important to observe John's use of the present and aorist tenses in his First Epistle. In I John 2:1 he uses the aorist twice with the verb *hamartanein,* to sin, *"My little children, I write these things to you in order that you won't even commit an act of sin* (aorist). *And, if anyone does commit a sin* (aorist), *we have an advocate with the Father."* In 3:9 he uses the present tense with the same verb: *"Everyone born of God does not practice or continue in sin* (present); *because his seed is abiding in him and he is not able to continue in sin–* . . . (present)."

Perfect Tense

The perfect tense in Greek is to my mind the most expressive. It expresses past completed action with presently continuing results. In John 17:10, our Lord speaks concerning his disciples ". . . I have been glorified in them." "Have been glorified" is in the Greek perfect tense, signifying "I have been glorified and continue to be glorified in them."

Imperfect Tense

The imperfect tense expresses durative or continuous action in past time. John 1:1, 2 has a telling example of this in the use of the verb *to be.* It translates literally like this, "In the beginning the Word *was* (imperfect tense, implying that he was already there in continuing existence) and the Word *was*

---

[1] Dana & Mantey, *Manual Grammar of the Greek New Testament* (New York: Macmillan, 1957), pg. 195.

with God (imperfect tense again, speaking of his continuing existence with God from the very beginning) and God *was* the Word (same imperfect tense, same import—the Word was always existing as God). (By the way, note the word order: *"God* was the Word," the emphasis being on the very nature of the Word). This one was (imperfect again—already in continuous existence) "in the beginning with God" (John 1:1, 2). Note the repetition of "in the beginning" for strong emphasis. We know from John 1:14 and 17 that "the Word" is Jesus Christ. The use of the imperfect tense in this passage is insisting on the fact that he *always was* (his eternal preexistence) and that he *always was deity,* and *he always was one of the Godhead.*

Future Tense

The Greek future tense, portraying action yet future, is roughly equivalent to our English future. However, since the event is yet future, and thus more or less uncertain, it reflects the "undefined" idea we see in the aorist, rather than continuity of action. A typical future is, "But the Counselor, the Holy Spirit, whom the Father *will send* (future tense) in my name, he *will teach* you all things . . . ."

There is one other tense, the pluperfect, which occurs so seldom in the New Testament we will not deal with it here. There are also distinctions of usage of each of the tenses which we will not attempt to treat. *A Manual Grammar of the Greek New Testament* by Dana and Mantey is a handbook of information which is very useful for study and reference. It is even useful to the English reader, even though it uses Greek words, for definitive data on Greek grammar and syntax.

Moods

Now, shifting our attention to *moods,* we are reminding you of a language feature that most of us have either forgotten or have never known. The mood (or mode) of a verb expresses the attitude of the writer or speaker with regard to the action. It can represent one of two viewpoints: (1) that which is actual and (2) that which is possible, like this:

Greek Moods

	Mood	Form	Meaning or Usage
ACTUAL	*Indicative*	*Declaration of fact—* reality	Verbal idea is actual—it *indicates* what is true about the subject
POSSIBLE	*Imperative*	*Command*—potential reality	Imposes a demand upon the will to do what is commanded, and is contingent upon the response.
	Subjunctive	*Contingency*—potentially possible	Expresses uncertainty. Used in exhortations and conditional clauses, where the action is objectively possible depending upon certain conditions and/ or responses.
	Optative	*Possibility*—conceivably possible	Expresses a wish or desire, often introduced by "*may.*"

The Indicative Mood

In English this is sometimes called the Declarative Mood, for by it the writer is stating a declaration of fact. In John 17:4 our Lord declares, addressing his Father in prayer, "I glorified thee" (aorist active indicative—pointing to this action viewed as a whole, which he is stating as an actual fact) "having accomplished work (aorist active participle which describes having fulfilled the assigned work) which thou gavest me to do . . . ." (perfect active indicative—which the Father gave him and still gives him, stated as a fact).

I hope I'm not moving too fast for you, for now we are viewing *tense, voice,* and *mood* together, plus an auxiliary verb form, the *participle*, which participates in the action of the main verb, describing, modifying or explaining its meaning.

The Imperative Mood

A rather startling use of the imperative is seen in 1 Thessalonians 5:

> And we exhort you, brethren, admonish the idle, encourage the fainthearted, help the weak, be patient with all of them, see that none of you repays evil for evil, but always seek to do good to one another and to all. Rejoice always, pray constantly, give thanks in all circumstances; for this is the will of God in Christ Jesus for you. Do not quench the Spirit, do not despise prophesying, but test everything; hold fast what is good, abstain from every form of evil . . . he who calls you is faithful, and he will do it (1 Thess. 5:14–22 & 24).

Did you notice the string of imperatives? *Admonish, encourage, help, be patient, see that none repays, seek to do good, rejoice, pray, give thanks, do not quench, do not despise, test, hold fast, abstain*—all make a demand on the will of the reader to obey the command. No light options, these! How we do it becomes another matter, but there is no mistaking the commands God issues through the apostle.

Sprinkled throughout the imperatives in this passage are a few indicative forms: *we beseech you,* in verse 12, a statement of fact making a strong plea for cooperation with God's design; and in verse 24, *he who calls you is faithful* (indicative —a fact) *and he will do it* (another indicative—it's a fact, but future tense—a promise he will prove true in time).

In the midst are two verbs in the *optative* mood, "may the God of peace himself sanctify you wholly; and may your spirit and soul and body be kept sound and blameless at the coming of our Lord Jesus Christ" (1 Thess. 5:23). *May . . . God*

. . . *sanctify you* (aorist active optative, expressing the wish or desire of the inspired apostle and thus of God himself). The same is true of *may your spirit and soul and body be kept sound and blameless.*

What a great deal we learn from these verb forms, especially their *mood.*

The Subjunctive Mood

Here is a feature of language almost lost in English, but very prominent in New Testament Greek. The subjunctive is the mood of uncertainty or contingency. In English we have a vestige of the subjunctive mood remaining in expressions like: *if I were king* using *were* instead of *was* to express a wish or condition which is not so in this case. In our English Bible it is seen often in the exhortations like, "Therefore *let us leave* the elementary doctrines of Christ *and go on* to maturity . . ." (Heb. 6:1). The words *let us* clue us in to the subjunctive mood, for the outcome is in doubt, contingent upon the response of the hearer to the appeal. Here, however, the Revised Standard Version loses the form of the initial verb in the Greek text; in this case, as in a number of others, the King James Version is better: "Therefore leaving the principles of the doctrine of Christ, *let us go on* to perfection." This translation carries over the verb *leaving* in its participial form and retains the subjunctive force of *let us go on* in its exhortation of the hearer. There is thus only one exhortation here, not two. This highlights the value, for English Bible students, of comparing translations, and for Greek students, the value of getting behind the English texts into the Greek New Testament. Other good key words of the English subjunctive are "should" and "might" when used as auxiliary verbs—"If I should go to the store . . ." "He came that we might have life."

The subjunctive mood also has significant usage in *condi-*

tional clauses. In John 1:8 and 9, for instance, we have several subjunctives: "If we say (subjunctive—maybe we do and maybe we don't; there is the possibility) we have no sin (indicative mood, assumed as a fact) we deceive ourselves (yes, you guessed it—indicative again) and the truth is not in us (another statement of fact, assuming we have said *we have no sin*). If we confess our sins (another subjunctive—maybe yes, maybe no) he is faithful and just, and will forgive our sin and cleanse us from all unrighteousness" (one indicative, *is faithful,* and two subjunctives, *will forgive* and *will cleanse,* implying that forgiveness and cleansing are contingent upon our confession but based on God's faithfulness to do what he promised). The one indicative form *he is faithful* stresses the *basis* of his being able to forgive and cleanse—the work of Christ, as in 1 John 1:7 ". . . the blood of Jesus his Son cleanses us from all unrighteousness."

Contextually, we need to recall that the issue here is *fellowship,* not salvation. Our enjoyment of life with God is at stake, not our possession of that life. Our salvation is based on the work of Christ which we appropriated when we invited him to be our Lord and Savior. Our fellowship (enjoying full participation in all that God has made available to us in his Son) is contingent upon our agreeing with him on the issues of our life—our walk with Christ and in Christ.

Conditional Clauses

At this point it should be noted that the conditional clauses cited above represent only one of four kinds the Greek uses. This one is the *truly conditional* clause which expresses the genuine contingency (maybe it's true and maybe it's not) in which the subjunctive mood is used to express that uncertainty based on the fact that the response could go either way. All four kinds are listed in the chart on the next page, com-

Greek Conditional Clauses

CLASS	EXPRESSION	IDENTIFICATION
First Class Condition	If . . . and it's true, or I am assuming it to be true for the purposes of my argument. The writer wishes to assume (or seem to assume) the reality of his premise.	*Ei*(if) used with any tense of the indicative, the mood of reality. e.g. "*If God is for us . . .*" (Rom. 8:31) and he is, as Paul has taken 8 chapters of Romans to prove. Could be translated "*Since God is for us . . .*" Here the reality of the premise is assumed, and is established by the context.
Second Class Condition	If . . . *and it's not true.* A contrary-to-fact condition or unfulfilled condition, e.g. John 11:32 "Lord, if you had been here . . ." (imperfect indicative) *but you were not.*	*Ei*(if) used with only the past tenses (aorist, imperfect or pluperfect) of the indicative mood. *Ei*(if) plus imperfect indicative = if . . . and it's not true about present. e.g. John 15:19,22, Gal. 1:10. *Ei*(if) plus aorist or pluperfect = if . . . and it's not true about past. e.g. John 11:32, Matt. 11:21, Mark 13:20
Third Class Condition	If . . . *and maybe it's true, maybe not.* A true condition, where the actual state is in doubt. e.g. 1 John 1:8–9 as explained previously.	*Ean* (if, implying uncertainty) used with the subjunctive, also implying uncertainty, leaving the issue in doubt. e.g. 1 John 1:8,9 cited previously.
Fourth Class Condition	Same as third class, with less probability of fulfillment.	*Ei* and *an* with the optative mood e.g. 1 Cor. 14:10, 15:37, 1 Peter 3:14.

prising an interesting and unusual (from our standpoint) feature of Greek.

Dana and Mantey, quoting A. T. Robertson, make a pertinent statement in regard to these expressive forms: "The point about all four classes to note is that the form of the condition has to do only with the statement, not with the absolute truth or certainty of the matter . . . we must distinguish always therefore between the fact and the statement of the fact. The conditional sentence deals only with the statement." [2]

For instance, the illustration I have given in the chart for a first class condition (Rom. 8:31) points up the reality of the fact that "God *is* for us," which is easy to see if we relate the conditional clause to the context. However, there are cases in which the conditional clause is *not* stating what is true, but rather the writer is assuming the premise stated in the conditional clause for the sake of his argument. This is the case with Galatians 2:21. "I do not nullify the grace of God; for *if righteousness comes through the Law* (a first class condition, assumed as true for the sake of the argument when it is *not really true*), then Christ died needlessly" (Gal. 2:21 NASV, italics mine). We see this same situation in 1 Corinthians. Paul writes in 1 Corinthians 15:15: "We are even found to be misrepresenting God, because we testify of God that he raised Christ, whom he did not raise *if it is true that the dead are not raised.*" (Here, first class condition assumed as true for the sake of the argument, when in fact the dead *are* raised.)

This is a bit tricky, but we can gain considerable understanding from conditional clauses if we take the time to think them through.

Voice

Voice is that property of the verbal idea which indicates how the subject is related to the action. In Greek, the active and passive voices are just like the English equivalents, but the Greek has an additional voice called the Middle Voice which has a reflexive force.

---

[2] Dana and Mantey, *Manual Grammar of the Greek New Testament* (New York: Macmillan, 1957), pp. 288–289.

Greek Voices

VOICE	THOUGHT	EXAMPLE
Active	The subject of the verb *produces* the action	"But God *shows* his love for us . . ." (Rom. 5:8).
Passive	The subject of the verb *receives* the action	". . . but you *were sanctified*, you *were justified* . . ." (1 Cor. 6:11).
Middle	The subject of the verb participates in the results of the action	"*He himself secured* eternal redemption" (Heb. 9:12).

Middle Voice

The middle voice is peculiarly Greek in its usage and defies exactness of translation into English. But we can understand several things about its various uses.

1. It refers the action back to the one acting. The action in some way reflects back upon the subject of the verb. It can have roughly the force of a reflexive pronoun as we would use it in English. For example, ". . . I *will myself be* a Father to him . . ." (Heb. 1:5, italics mine) in which the verb *will be* is in the middle voice.

2. It can have the force of emphasizing the part taken by the subject of the verb as in ". . . *having by himself* made a cleansing of sins . . ." (Heb. 1:3, literal translation, italics mine).

3. It can represent the subject as voluntarily yielding himself to the action of the verb, e.g., "Why not *let yourselves* be wronged?" (1 Cor. 6:7, literal translation, italics mine).

Perhaps these examples are enough to give the flavor of the middle voice. Your own investigations of its specific use can, I hope, lead you to the local significance as you encounter its use in the Greek text of the New Testament.

Prepositions

Though they are usually very small words, a great deal of meaning can be determined by their usage. The diagram and chart which follow will illustrate how far-reaching their effects can be.

Diagram of the Directive and Local Functions of Prepositions

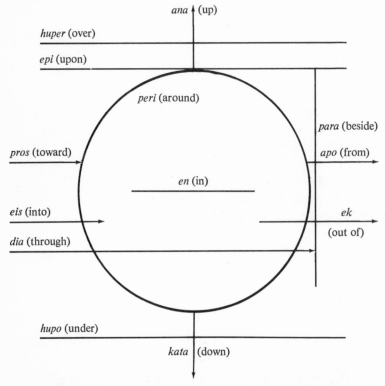

(From Dana and Mantey, *Manual Grammar of the Greek New Testament*)

Prepositional Meanings Classified

	Direction	Position	Relation	Agency	Means	Cause	Association	Purpose
ana	up	in, by						
anti			in exchange for, instead of, for			because of		
apo	from		for	by		on account of		
dia	through		for	by	through, by means of	because of		for the sake of
ek	out of	on			by means of	because of		
en	into	in, on, at, within	besides, among	in	with, by means of	because of	with	
eis	into, unto, to	in, among, upon	as, for, against, in respect to			because of		for the purpose of
epi	up to, to	upon, at, on, in, by, before, over	against, after, in the time of			on account of		for
kata	along, down, upon, throughout	down, from, upon, at, in, by, before	according to, with reference to					
meta			after				with	
para	beyond, to the side of, from	beside, before	contrary to				with	
peri	around, about		in behalf of, concerning, about				with	
pro		before						
pros	to, toward	at, on, beside	against, for, pertaining to		by means of	on account of	with	for
sun			besides				with	
liuper	beyond	over, above	concerning, for, instead of, on behalf of					for the sake of
hupo		under		by				

(From Dana and Mantey, *Manual Grammar of the Greek Testament*).

I have found this chart so helpful that I have put it in the flyleaf of my Bible. To illustrate how important prepositions can be, I would like to cite two glaring cases of careless (and thus faulty) translation. In the Revised Standard Version John 13:8 reads, "If I do not wash you, you have no part *in* me." The Greek preposition translated "in" is *meta,* which should be translated *"with."* The King James Version and the New American Standard properly translate it so. The difference is crucial! "In me" would indicate that Peter's salvation was in question, whereas "with me" speaks of Peter's fellowship with Christ—his joint participation with the Lord in the activities of life.

The other faulty translation is perhaps just as costly if we fail to get the true meaning inferred from the prepositions used. It is in Ephesians 4:11, 12, and here even the New American Standard Version doesn't keep it straight. The passage should read, if we observe the Greek prepositions used: "And he gave some prophets, some evangelists, some pastors and teachers *toward* (Greek, *pros*) the equipping of the saints *unto* (Greek, *eis*) the work of ministry, *unto* (Greek, *eis*) the building of the body of Christ . . ." (italics mine).

Most of the translations fail to make the distinction between the prepositions used here in the Greek text. Thus it obscures the fact that the ministry belongs to *all* God's people, not just the pastor-teachers. The result of this failure has, among other things, contributed greatly to the Christian "unemployment" problem. Many Christians would think themselves to be presumptuous to entertain the idea of having a ministry for the Lord.

In his *Practical Use of the Greek New Testament* Kenneth Wuest resolves a seeming contradiction by translating a single preposition properly:

A careful study of the Greek preposition discloses some precious truth that would otherwise be obscured by reason of a wrong interpretation put upon an English preposition, and at the same time saves the expositor from arriving at a wrong interpretation.

Take the difficult statement in Matthew 3:11, "I indeed baptize you with water unto repentance." The word "unto" means "result." For instance, "For I am not ashamed of the gospel, . . . for it is the power of God unto (resulting in) salvation" (Rom. 1:16) Are we to understand that a person's submission to water baptism results in his repentance? That is exactly what the Authorized Version says.

The Greek student will find that the preposition *eis* appears in Matthew 3:11 and Romans 1:16. But prepositions in Greek are not confined to a single meaning in every context. Nor are they to be translated in a uniform way in their every occurrence in the Greek text.

A *preposition* has *root* meanings, *resultant* meanings, and *remote* meanings. It also has special meanings when used in composition with verbal forms. When the student is confronted with a problem like this, he should consult Dana and Mantey on the word *eis*. These scholars have classified the various uses of the prepositions in the New Testament. They also give illustrations of their various usages. For instance they give "they repented at the preaching of Jonah" (Matt. 12:41). Of course, one would not translate, "They (the men of Nineveh) repented unto the preaching of Jonah." That is, it would be ridiculous to say that the preaching of Jonah was the result of the repentance of the Ninevites. It was the other way round. They repented *because of* the preaching of Jonah. The Greek student would say here that this usage of *eis* would fit the context in which Matthew 3:11 is found. It would agree with the teaching of other scriptures regarding the significance of water baptism. He would translate, "I indeed baptize you with water *because* of repentance." That is, repentance precedes water baptism, and baptism is the outward visible testimony of an inward fact, the person's repentance. Thus, another problem is solved, a difficulty removed, and an erroneous translation corrected, upon which translation is built the false doctrine of baptismal regeneration. We have the same difficulty in Acts. 1:38. The same Greek preposition is used, and the same solution will meet the problem.[3]

---

[3] Kenneth Wuest, *Practical Use of the Greek New Testament* (Chicago: Moody Press, n.d.), p. 61 and 62.

Word Studies

A productive interpretive exercise is to use the Greek lexicon to arrive at a deeper or clearer meaning of words than our English translations give. A most revealing example of this kind of vocabulary study is contained in the Greek text of Romans: "And do not be conformed to this world, but be transformed by the renewing of your mind . . ." (Rom. 12:2 NASV) In this verse we have "conformed" and "transformed" in the English text. "Conformed" is a translation of the Greek verb *suschematizo,* "to form with." Vine's *Expository Dictionary of New Testament Words* tells us *suschematizo* refers "to that which is transitory, changeable, unstable, and it *could not be used of inward transformation"* (Vine, p. 227).

"Transformed" is a translation of the Greek verb *metamorphoō,* and Vine, speaking of *morphé,* from which it is formed, says this with particular reference to Philippians 2:5–11. (The verse referred to here is Philippians 2:6):

> An excellent definition of the word is that of Gifford: *"morphé is therefore properly the nature or essense,* not in the abstract, but as actually subsisting in the individual, and retained as long as the individual itself exists . . . Thus in the passage before us *morphe Theou* is the Divine nature actually and inseparably subsisting in the Person of Christ. . . . *[4]*

Schēma is described this way:

> *Schēma,* a figure, fashion (akin to *echō,* to have), is translated "fashion" in I Corinthians 7:31, of the world, signifying that which comprises the manner of life, actions, etc., of humanity in general; in Phil. 2:8 it is used of the Lord in His being found "in fashion" as a man, and signifies *what He was in the eyes of men,* "the entire outwardly perceptible mode and shape of His existence, just as the preceding words *morphē,* form,

---

[4] W. E. Vine, *Expository Dictionary of New Testament Words* (Old Tappan, N.J.: Fleming H. Revell Co., n.d.), p. 23.

and *homoiōma,* likeness, describe what He was in Himself as Man" (Gifford on the Incarnation, p. 44). "Men saw in Christ a human form, bearing, language, action, mode of life . . . in general the state and relations of a human being, so that in the entire mode of His appearance He made Himself known and was recognized as a man" (Meyer).[5]

So, what have we learned? Looking back to Romans 12:2, to paraphrase the verse, "Do not let yourself be formed into the world's pattern by its transient external pressures, but rather be permanently changed from within by the renewing of your mind . . . ." And if you recall Titus 3:5, that "renewing" is by the Holy Spirit. The idea is that we do not just put on an outward show of change, but we undergo a deep, abiding change in our innermost being. Phillips' translation then shines with considerable brilliance as it reflects the meaning of the Greek.

> With eyes wide open to the mercies of God, I beg you, my brothers, as an act of intelligent worship, to give him your bodies, as a living sacrifice, consecrated to him and acceptable by him. *Don't let the world around you squeeze you into its own mold, but let God re-make you so that your whole attitude of mind is changed.* Thus you will prove in practice that the will of God's good, acceptable to him and perfect (Rom. 12:1,2, italics mine).

One more example: let us check the use of the word *nature* in the New Testament. If we were to rely solely on the English texts we would be somewhat misled, for the translators sometimes translate the Greek word *anthropos,* meaning *man,* by the word "nature." This is done in the Revised Standard Version of Colossians 3:9 and 10, where *old nature* and *new nature* are really *old man* and *new man.* This is misleading, for the Greek word for nature is *phusis,* and it only occurs some sixteen times in the New Testament, if we count noun, adverbial, and adjectival forms. These occurrences are Romans

[5] Ibid., p. 79.

1:26, 1:27, 2:14, 2:27, 11:21, 11:24; 1 Corinthians 11:14; Galatians 2:15 & 4:8; Ephesians 2:3; James 3:7; 2 Peter 1:4, 2:12 and Jude 10.

You may say, so what? Well, it doesn't seem to mean much until we do a study on the nature of man. Does the Christian have one nature or two? From our English translations and from what many have taught on this subject it would appear that we have *two* natures. But if we seriously consider the use of the word *phusis* as meaning nature in the sense of doing what comes naturally and being what we are, then we must review our thinking.

Phusis is used in Galatians 2:15 of those who are "Jews by nature." Certainly it is not possible to be both Jews by nature and Gentiles by nature at the same time. It's either one or the other, not both. If we turn from this thought to the *one* occasion in the New Testament where *phusis* is used of Christians we read, "that by them you might became partakers of the *divine nature* . . ." (2 Peter 1:4 NASV, italics mine). So I conclude that the Christian only has *one nature*. It is now, since I am in Christ and no longer in Adam, as natural for me to be like Christ as it was previously natural for me to be ungodly. And our expectancy is exactly that, even though our experience sometimes falls short. It's interesting how clearly we expect godly behavior from Christians. Even the world expects us to behave better when we are in Christ! When we do badly even we ourselves consider it a *lapse* from the norm—not the norm.

What practical use has this view of the nature of man? Well, for one thing it forces me to stop making room for sin and excusing myself with, "I'm only human after all." And that's progress. But so that we don't misconstrue, this doesn't mean I will never sin again, either. God makes this clear in 1 John 1:8–10, so that if I say, "I have no sin," I only fool myself. What God's Word is saying in all this is that though I cannot say I *will* never sin again, I can say I *need not* sin again. Why?

Because I have God's nature now, and any actions that would indicate the contrary are just part of my Adamic hangover. After all, I trained the flesh quite well before I knew Christ.

To conclude, if you want to talk about "old nature" and "new nature" just remember the old one is "old" in the sense that *it used to belong to you, but no more.* You only have one *new* nature. Now it is natural for you to be Christlike!

I hope these suggestions make you eager to understand some of the "untranslatable riches" that God has implanted in the Greek of the New Testament.

□ 11 □

Helpful Hints on Hebrew

The only Hebrew I know, as the saying goes, is the man who has the tailor shop around the corner. And this doesn't help much toward understanding the Hebrew language, because usually he doesn't know it either. But *Strong's Exhaustive Concordance* comes to my rescue for whatever I, personally, can gain of the meaning of Hebrew terms.

Strong's is a listing of every word in the Bible in the main concordance section, with a Hebrew/Chaldee dictionary and a Greek dictionary in the back of the book. Though there are other features in it, these are the significantly useful parts. Many people think a concordance is only for locating a verse in the Bible, and certainly it is useful toward that end. But the dictionary sections have proved to be the most useful to me, particularly the Hebrew dictionary, for it is the only way I have to enter into some of the Old Testament word meanings.

All except a small portion of the Old Testament was written in Hebrew, but Jeremiah 10:11, Daniel 2:4 to 7:28 and Ezra 4:8–6:18 and 7:12–26 were evidently recorded in the Chaldean (or Aramaic) language. It is closely related to Hebrew, but different, I am told. The purpose for this change of language in these Old Testament books is beautifully illustrated in Daniel. To quote from Terry's *Biblical Hermeneutics:*

Daniel, who received an early and thorough training in the tongue of the Chaldeans, is the first biblical writer who formally employs this dialect in sacred composition. After having narrated in Hebrew the successful training of himself and his three companions, he passes in the second chapter to an account of Nebuchadnezzar's dream, and from verse 4, where the Chaldeans begin their address to the king: "O king, forever live!" This being the very language in which all the conversation of the court was carried on, its use here gives to Daniel's narrative a life-like reality, and is a monumental evidence of the genuineness and authenticity of the record. Only a writer of Daniel's time and position, and bilinguous as he was, would have written thus. Nebuchadnezzar's dream was a God-given vision of world empire, and of its final overthrow by the power and kingdom of God; and the dream and its interpretation were written down in a language then common alike to the people of God and to the mightiest empire of the world. The succeeding narratives of the golden image and the deliverance of Daniel's three companions (chapter 4), Belshazzar's feast and sudden overthrow (chapter 5), and Daniel's deliverance from the lions' den (chapter 6) were also recorded in the language of the empire, for they were written for the world to know . . . but when, in the eighth chapter, the prophet passes to visions of more special import to his own people, he resumes in Hebrew.[1]

Using Strong's Concordance

So our concordance has a Hebrew/Chaldee dictionary, but how does one make use of it? Let me illustrate one way we can use it. In Genesis 11:26 I encounter the name "Abram" for the first time, and in Genesis 17:5 I see that God changes his name to "Abraham."

No longer shall your name be Abram, but your name shall be Abraham; for I have made you the father of a multitude of nations (Gen. 17:5).

---

[1] Milton S. Terry, *Biblical Hermeneutics* (Grand Rapids: Zondervan Publishing House, n.d.), p. 109.

So I sense there is meaning in both of these names, and my curiosity leads me to check the Hebrew dictionary in Strong's Concordance. I look under *Abram* in the main concordance section (on page 12) and find under Genesis 17:5 the verse I'm checking with a number 87 on the right hand margin. This is a reference number to the Hebrew dictionary (page 8) in the back of the book. So I turn there, making sure I don't mistake it for the Greek dictionary adjoining it (which has the numbers italicized to distinguish it from the Hebrew dictionary), and I find this:

"*Abram,* ab-rawm; contr. (contraction) from 48; *high father; Abram,* the original name of Abraham."

I check 48 on the previous page to see the longer form of the word, meaning the same, *high father.* I follow the same procedure with *Abraham* and find under 85 on page 8 of the Hebrew dictionary:

"*Abraham,* ab-raw-hawm; contraction from 1 and an unused root (probably meaning *to be populous*); *father of a multitude.*"

Then I turn back to 1 (on page 7) and find that *ab* is a primary word meaning *father.* So I have learned a little Hebrew, and returning to the verse I'm investigating, I observe that this little bit of research correlates with the explanatory clause, "for I have made you the father of a multitude of nations" in Genesis 17:5.

You say, "I could have understood that much from the English text," and it's true that sometimes our research doesn't add much to our understanding. But then, when we come to ". . . *Abba, father* . . ." in Romans 8:15 we are able to recognize that Paul is lapsing back into his familiar Hebrew (or Aramaic) vocabulary which takes the mystery out of *Abba.* However, the real value of the study of this word shows up when we read God's promise to Abraham:

> Indeed I will greatly bless you, and I will greatly multiply your seed as the stars of heaven and as the sand which is on

the seashore . . . and in your seed all the nations of the earth shall be blessed . . . (Gen. 22:17,18 NASV).

Here we see how his name Abraham (father of a multitude) really applies. By implication his will be an earthly family (depicted by "sand"), a heavenly family (depicted by "stars"), and universal blessing to all nations through his seed which is Christ (see Gal. 3:16 NASV). For even further emphasis we find the same promise repeated in Genesis 15:5 and restated to Isaac and Jacob in Genesis 26:4 and 32:12. So our investigation of the Hebrew meaning of Abraham's name really pays off. He is indeed "father of a multitude," both physically and spiritually.

I have outlined this simple, step-by-step procedure because I have found that many do not know the availability of this information in the concordance, or how to dig it out. And though the rewards may be minimal on some occasions at other times we will discover a wealth of information.

For other salient features of the Hebrew, I have turned to my dear friend and fellow-pastor, David Roper, who is a real "pro" on biblical Hebrew. Listen to what he has to say regarding this phase of Bible interpretation. And I'll be learning along with you, for this data will be new to me, too.

What Every Bible Student Needs to Know about Hebrew
by
David H. Roper

The books of the Old Testament, as I'm sure you've been told, were written mainly in Hebrew. There are, however, some short sections set down in the Aramaic language, as Bob Smith has already pointed out.

Aramaic occurs in the Old Testament because it was the language of the Jewish exiles. From the seventh century B.C. on it was the official court language first of the Babylonian and then of the Persian Empires. It is understandable, then, why Aramaic occurs in books that have their setting in the period when the Jews were exiled from their land. It is important to know, however, that although Hebrew and Aramaic are different languages they are in the same family—the Semitic language group—and thus have many common characteristics. (Grammarians describe them as "cognate" languages because they share a common parent language.) For practical purposes, then, we can view them in the same way. When we refer to the Hebrew language in this study, we are, in effect, referring to the language of the Old Testament.

Semitic Languages

Since we've raised the issue of a family of languages to which Hebrew is related, it might be helpful to elaborate on this connection. To do so explains, for example, how the patriarchs could communicate so freely with the native population of Canaan. That communication is clearly indicated in the Old Testament. You may have wondered about it yourself. The answer is actually quite simple—they all spoke essentially the same language. There were dialectical differences, to be sure, but the evidence from the ancient literature sources of Israel's neighbors (the Phoenicians, Moabites, Canaanites, and so on) indicates that they all used Canaanite dialects closely related to Hebrew and they could have communicated without any significant language barrier.

The family of Semitic languages is usually divided into three groups, according to their geographical distribution: Northeast Semitic, Southwest Semitic and Northwest Semitic. The Northeast Semitic branch is called Akkadian and, generally speaking, was the language of the Assyrians and Babylonians, and the Southwest branch embraces Arabic. The Northwest Semitic language group is by far the largest, comprising the previously mentioned *Aramaic* language that was originally spoken in Aramea (later Syria) and a number of dialects usually termed *Canaanite*. The people in Phoenicia, Canaan, Edom, Moab, and, apparently, even portions of Sinai, all used some form of this Canaanite language.

It may surprise you to learn that Hebrew is derived from the Canaanite branch of the Northwest Semitic family. In fact, Hebrew is called in the Bible the "language of Canaan" (Isa. 19:18). We do not know what language the patriarch Abraham spoke when he came from Haran (we can reasonably assume it was an early form of Aramaic) but, apparently, after settling in Canaan he adopted the local Canaanite dialect which became the basis for Israel's national language.

What this means, then, is that Hebrew belongs to an extensive language family spoken throughout the near East from Syria to the Sinai Peninsula and from the Mediterranean Sea to Mesopotamia. Furthermore, since all the nations in this region were bound together linguistically, we should expect to find other cultural and literary parallels, and indeed they do exist. All these so-called Semitic peoples were, in fact, united by a more or less common culture. Israel, as a nation, did not stand in cultural isolation, nor did her literature. There are thousands of documents from the near East that have some bearing on our understanding of the language of the Old Testament; new meanings for rare biblical words are being discovered and many obscure references are being cleared up. And this information is increasingly available even to the nonspecialist. We'll refer to some of these sources later.

Hebrew Thought Patterns

The difficult thing about Hebrew from our perspective is simply that it is a Semitic or Eastern language, quite different from any of the Indo-European languages familiar to us. Most of us here in the West have at least dabbled around with Spanish, Latin, or French in our school days, but unless we've taken an Arabic language course we've never encountered anything quite like Hebrew. Certainly the script is peculiar. It reads from right to left, and there are a host of other rather obvious disparities. However, the real difference is less obvious, and it is this difference that is the real crux of the matter: *Hebrew is a vehicle for expressing a uniquely Eastern viewpoint.* The problem then, is not merely one of understanding another language, but of understanding another way of looking at life and things. It is this point that most English readers do not fully appreciate. There are many specialized language tools which can be used to define terms and better understand nuances of meaning, but these in themselves are inadequate, simply because they can't reproduce this cultural dimension. In fact, I don't know that it can be adequately reproduced. The only way to fully understand a people is to get fully involved in their language, literature, and customs. Unfortunately, that just isn't possible for most folks. Few have the time or inclination to learn the requisite number of dead Semitic languages and then immerse themselves in the literature. (Some who did, it appears, never came up!) There are, however, some basic perspectives which, when maintained, will enable anyone to more fully appreciate and more accurately interpret the Old Testament. These, I believe, are as follows:

1. *A Different Way of Looking at an Action*

Hebrew verb tenses are odd things—at least they are from our point of view. They made perfectly good sense to the Semite-on-the-street, I'm sure, but, apparently, they were more concerned with the *mode* or *manner* of an action rather than the time when it occurred. Or to put it another way, they were not so much interested in *when* an action took place as in its *state of completion*—whether it was complete or incomplete. Properly speaking, then, Hebrew verb tenses are not tenses at all. They rather indicate "aspect" (a phase of action) as the grammarians say. In English we usually think in terms of strict time sequences. If I say, "I went to Oregon on my vacation," any English-speaking person hearing these words would understand that the action occurred in the past; not so the Hebrew, however. He evidently did not think in those strict categories. He could view that action as completed (and thus *perhaps* in the past), or still going on, or not yet begun, but apparently nothing beyond those aspects of action mattered! Let's see how it works.

Hebrew Perfect and Imperfect Verbs

Hebrew verbs indicate two "aspects" of action. The Hebrew *perfect* viewed the action as complete; the *imperfect* represented it as incomplete, repetitive or continual. Normally the translators render the Hebrew perfect as an English past tense and the imperfect as an English present or future tense. There is really no other way to handle the problem in translation, but we have to understand that the Hebrew author was not thinking in those strict, temporal categories. For the Hebrew the action was complete or incomplete; time was almost irrelevant, and that is the way we have to learn to view the action. For example, Genesis 12:1 reads, "Now the Lord *said* to Abram, 'Go from your country'. . . ." That verse has occasioned a lot of controversy because of a supposed conflict with Stephen's statement in Acts 7:3 indicating that this call occurred *before* he migrated to Haran. The Genesis passage, on the other hand, makes it appear that the call came *after* he reached Haran. Once you understand the Hebrew verb system, however, the apparent conflict vanishes. The point of the statement in Genesis 12:1 is simply that the action *occurred*. It was completed at some point in time—the actual sequence of events is irrelevant. We could, therefore, translate the verb as an English pluperfect, "The Lord *had said* to Abram . . ." and make perfectly good sense out of the sequence of events. There are, of course, numerous examples in the Old Testament, since almost every sentence contains at least one verb, but perhaps you've seen enough now to gain a general impression. The important question to ask yourself in each case is, "What *aspect* of action does the author have in mind?"

But There's More to It . . .

One qualifying note: To clarify this matter I have vastly oversimplified it. The Hebrew verb is actually far more complex than I've presented it. At times, for example, the Old Testament writers, contrary to expectations, will indicate a *future* action by employing a *perfect tense verb*. They do so when they intend to represent these future actions as completed *in the thought of the speaker*. In other words, they *conceive* those actions as accomplished fact though *the action has not yet taken place*. Numbers 17:12 is a good example: "The people of Israel said to Moses, 'Behold, we have perished, we have died, *we have all died'* " (literal translation). In other words in their mind they were as good as dead. We would say, "We are done for." This same idiom occurs in contracts and treaty stipulations, i.e., Genesis 23:11, "I give you the field," (though the field was not yet in Abraham's possession) and especially in promises made by God (Genesis 15:18, "To your descendants *I have given* this land" literal translation).

The most vivid use of this verb form is in the prophetic material, where the event or scene which the prophet describes is depicted as having already been realized. In his mind the event, though yet future, is deemed "as good as done." For example, Isaiah 5:13 literally reads, "My people *have gone* into captivity" (obviously they had not in Isaiah's time).

English readers may find it difficult to identify these "prophetic perfects" from our English translations. However, you should be aware of this grammatical feature since it can occasionally affect our interpretation of prophetic statements. At times the translator may inadvertently mistranslate one of these verbs to indicate action in past time. The impression, thus, is that this is an action which has already occurred—as if it were an historical event, whereas in fact it is not. It is a *prediction,* but the prophet sees it existing in the future in a completed state. Isaiah 10:28–32 is a case in point.

> He has come against Aiath,
> He has passed through Migron;
> At Michmash he deposited his baggage,
> They have gone through the pass, saying,
> "They have made a lodging place in Geba."
> Ramah is terrified, and Gibeah of Saul has fled away.
> Cry aloud with your voice, O daughter of Gallim!
> Pay attention, Laishah and wretched Anathoth!
> Madmenah has fled.
> The inhabitants of Gebim have sought refuge.
> Yet today he will halt at Nob;
> He shakes his fist at the mountain of the daughter
> of Zion, the hill of Jerusalem (Isa. 10:28–32 NASV).

Most translations take these verbs in the past tense. It is obvious, however, from the context, that the action is yet future. Isaiah is predicting the line of march which an invading army (Assyria) will take on their trek southward to beseige Jerusalem, an event yet future from Isaiah's standpoint, yet the attack is so certain in the prophet's mind that he treats it as an accomplished fact. Even without a knowledge of Hebrew you should be able, in most cases, to spot this prophetic use of the perfect. *Any past tense verb in a context of future tense verbs may be a prophetic perfect.* You should at least consider that possibility. In the passage mentioned above, for example (Isa. 10:28–32), the verb in the paragraphs before and after are in the imperfect and thus are translated as English future tenses. The abrupt shift in tense at verse 28 should tip you off to the presence of this feature. Watch for it.

2. *Understanding Hebrew Sentence Formation*

Sentence formation in ancient Hebrew was, as the grammarians say, paratactic. By that they mean that the Hebrew simply connected whole strings of sentences using the conjunction "and." This literal translation of Genesis 1:1 is a good example of this tendency: "In the beginning God created the heavens and the earth *and* the earth was without form and void *and* darkness was on the face of the deep *and* the spirit of God was brooding over the waters *and* God said 'let there be light *and* there was light. . . .' " Only rarely did they subordinate clauses or phrases as we do in English. Ancient Hebrew did possess various articles capable of expressing precise subordinate relationships (the conjunctions "in order that," or "but" occur, for example), but for the most part the simple "and" served to convey those ideas.

As a connective between clauses "and" may mean simply "and" (if the idea of clause A is *coordinate* with the idea of clause B) or "but" (if the idea of B stands in *opposition* to that of A), or "in order that" (if B explains the *purpose* of), or "so that" (if B is the *result* of A) or "while" (if B is the *attendant circumstance* of A), and so on.

In other words the "and" in Hebrew simply operated as a plus sign, linking idea B with idea A and left it to the reader to put them in proper relationship to one another. There is even some recent thinking that the Hebrew "and" is not a conjunction at all but simply a way of introducing the next idea —a "presentative" they call it—like the French "voila" ("behold!" or "here it is!"). For example, in Hebrew, all the following sentences are, connected by "and." Yet note what a variety of relationships can be expressed in these literal translations:

> Elijah went to show himself to Ahab *when* (and) the famine became severe in Samaria. (1 Kings 18:2)

> Oh Lord, you have searched me *so that* (and) you know me intimately (Ps. 139:1).

> He (the servant of the Lord) was oppressed *even though* (and) he was submissive (Hebrew: "bowed down") (Isa. 53:7).

Again, we could multiply examples, but perhaps these verses are enough to give you some understanding of this grammatical feature and a new way of looking at sentence structure. When you see "and" in an Old Testament text, learn to look for other possibilities. In some cases the translators may have linked two thoughts as coordinate sentences when in actual fact some other relationship is intended. Ask yourself: Can I insert here "but," "so that," "in order that," "when," "while," or other subordinating conjunctions? That question may lead you to a new and significant insight.

3. *Understanding Evocative Imagery*

Hebrew is a language rich in imagery. The Semitic people in general were not given to abstract definition and precise delineation of ideas, but rather to eloquent symbolism and imagery. The language was, therefore, a powerful medium for touching and moving the emotions. Hebrew lacks the ability of most Indo-European languages to express subtle shades of meaning. For instance, Latin is far more concise and thus the proper medium for legal terminology, while Greek is better suited to the delicate shades of theological meaning found in the New Testament. But Hebrew has a force of its own—a remarkable ability to evoke enduring mental images by use of powerful symbols. It's this characteristic that I call *evocative imagery*. The images in the Old Testament come from a number of sources but are drawn principally from the physical features of the Near East (the flora, fauna, and topography of that region); the customs and habits of the people (cf. Jer. 2:13; Isa. 5:1,2; 40:26); and Israelite or pagan worship.

It may surprise you to learn that some of the most powerful symbols are taken right out of pagan cult terminology and from their myths and legends. For example, the sea monster frequently referred to in the Old Testament and variously named (Rahab, Leviathan, Tannin, and so on) is taken directly from Near Eastern mythology (See Mary K. Wakeman's

God's Battle with the Monster, a Study in Biblical Imagery). The *theology* of the Old Testament, of course, is radically different from that of pagan literature, but many of the symbols and figures are shared in common.

Be aware of this characteristic in the Old Testament and try to focus on the *image* that the writer wishes to convey instead of the specific details of the passage. It's not that the details are unimportant; every aspect of scripture has its own importance. However, there is a big picture being painted and you ought to stand back and look at the whole in order to grasp the full intent of the author.

For example, note this lovely lyric interlude in Isaiah's prophecy:

> When the poor and needy seek water,
>> and there is none,
>> and their tongue is parched with thirst,
> I the Lord will answer them,
>> I the God of Israel will not forsake them.
> I will open rivers on the bare heights,
>> and fountains in the midst of the valleys;
> I will make the wilderness a pool of water,
>> and the dry land springs of water.
> I will put in the wilderness the cedar,
>> the acacia, the myrtle, and the olive;
> I will set in the desert the cypress,
>> the plane and the pine together;
> that men may see and know,
>> may consider and understand together,
> that the hand of the Lord has done this,
>> the Holy One of Israel has created it (Isa. 41:17–20).

Can you picture this scene in your mind? It's clear, I believe, what Isaiah is saying about God's provision for the exiles' needs. Truth graphically portrayed in this way has an intensity and emotional impact that mere words or abstractions could never produce. As another example note Isaiah's description of the fall of Babylon:

Behold, the day of the Lord comes,
  cruel, with wrath and fierce anger,
to make the earth a desolation
  and to destroy its sinners from it.
For the stars of the heavens and their
    constellations
  will not give their light;
the sun will be dark at its rising
  and the moon will not shed its light.
I will punish the world for its evil,
  and the wicked for their iniquity;
I will put an end to the pride of the arrogant,
  and lay low the haughtiness of the ruthless.
I will make men more rare than fine gold,
  and mankind than the gold of Ophir.
Therefore, I will make the heavens tremble,
  and the earth will be shaken out of its place,
  at the wrath of the Lord of hosts
  in the day of his fierce anger.
And like a hunted gazelle,
  or like sheep with none to gather them,
  every man will turn to his own people,
    and every man will flee to his own land.
Whoever is found will be thrust through,
  and whoever is caught will fall by the sword.
Their infants will be dashed in pieces
  before their eyes;
their houses will be plundered
  and their wives ravished (Isa. 13:9–16).

Babylon fell in 539 B.C., so this is a prophecy which has been historically fulfilled and thus we have a reference point for interpreting the imagery. The cosmic disorder described here did not actually occur—at least there are no historical references to the heavens trembling and the earth being shaken out of its orbit. Instead, we see that the intent of the author is not to give a precise description of events but rather to paint a vivid mental image of the political and personal upheaval and turmoil that accompanied the fall of Babylon. Learn to "see" the Old Testament in this way.

4. *Interpreting Symbols and Figures of Speech*

A characteristic closely related to evocative imagery is the extensive use of figures of speech in the Old Testament. No language has a word for every idea. That's one of the weaknesses of language, and biblical Hebrew in particular suffers in this regard, since it has such a limited vocabulary. In addition, there is, as we have indicated, a tendency in Hebrew to express ideas symbolically rather than abstractly. Thus, the authors of the Old Testament rely extensively on figurative language. We must therefore learn to recognize some of their frequently-employed figures of speech. Some of these have been mentioned previously, but their application to Old Testament Hebrew is particularly significant.

a) *Euphemism*—the substitution of an inoffensive or mild expression for one that might offend or suggest something unpleasant.

Isaiah 57:8—"You loved their bed. Their 'hand' you gazed at" (for illicit sexual desire).

b) *Metonymy*—the use of a concrete term for another more abstract idea.

Isaiah 22:22—"Then I will set the key (way to gain access) of David on his *shoulder* . . ." (as a burden, or heavy responsibility).

c) *Synechdoche*—a use of the whole for a part or a part for the whole.

Isaiah 53:10—"If he would render up his *soul* (himself) as a guilt offering . . . ."

d) *Merism*—a form of synechdoche where a totality is expressed by two opposites.

Genesis 1:1—"In the beginning God created the *heavens* and the *earth*" (i.e., the universe).

e) *Personification*—The representation of inanimate objects or abstract objects as endowed with personal attributes.

Isaiah 35:1—"The *wilderness* and the *desert* shall be glad. . . ."

f) *Apostrophe*—a turning away from one's audience to address directly a person or thing, or an abstract idea or imaginary object (frequent in prophetic books).

g) *Hyperbole*—an exaggeration used for emphasis.

Isaiah 34:1–17 (Description of the destruction of nations).

h) *Irony*—The intended implication is opposite the literal meaning of the words.

Isaiah 41:23 (Addressed to idols)—"Indeed, do good or evil that *we may anxiously look about us and fear.*"

j) *Simile*—one thing, action or relationship is explicitly compared with something else ("as" or "like").

k) *Metaphor*—a word or phrase used in place of another to suggest a likeness or analogy.

Isaiah 1:10—"Hear the word of the Lord, you rulers of Sodom (Jerusalem)."

l) *Hendiadys*—a stylistic device in which two coordinate terms are joined by "and" to convey a single concept.

Genesis 3:16—"I will greatly multiply your *pain* and *childbirth*" (i.e. "painful childbirth").

m) *Anthropomorphism*—the representation of God in the form of, or with the attributes of, a man.

Isaiah 7:18—"And it shall come about that the Lord will *whistle* for the fly which is at the sources of the rivers of Egypt."

n) *Anthropopathism*—the ascription to God of the emotions and passions of man.

Psalm 2:4—"He who sits in the heavens will *laugh.*"

o) *Zoomorphism*—the representation of God in the form of, or with the attributes of, the lower animals.

Psalm 63:7—"In the shadow of thy *wings* I sing for joy."

There are other less frequently used symbols in the Old Testament. E. W. Bullinger's *Figures of Speech Used in the Bible* (Baker Book House) will give you a more complete listing. Those listed here, however, are the figures of speech you will encounter most often in the Old Testament and, once understood, will give you a greater appreciation for the Hebrew mind and the image-producing faculty of the Hebrew language. Again, you need to bear in mind that the purpose of the author is to produce a vivid mental picture rather than convey a merely abstract concept. Keeping that purpose in mind will prevent you from going beyond the intent of the author.

Now for a word about *words* and how to define them. Unfortunately, there are fewer tools in Hebrew for the nonspecialist than there are in Greek, but there are some available and you should learn how to use them. They can help you get beyond the English translations to the meaning of the Hebrew texts underlying them. They are:

1) *Strong's Exhaustive Concordance of the Bible*

An exhaustive concordance of the Bible contains every word found in the Bible and indicates where each word occurs. Strong's concordance is based on the *English text* and more particularly that of the Authorized Version (King James Version). It's really very simple to use and correctly utilized can give you a richer understanding of any word found in scripture. For example, let's look at a term taken from another of Isaiah's prophecies, the well-known "Suffering Servant" passage in Isaiah 53. Verse 53:5 reads in part: "But he was wounded for our transgressions, he was bruised for our iniquities." If we wanted to know the meaning of the term "wounded" we could look up the word in Strong's Concordance; it occurs on page 1192. Under the entry "wounded" we would find the clause containing that word by Isaiah 53:5. In the right hand column we'd find a number (in this case 2490) which would be found in the "Hebrew and Chaldee Dictionary" at the back of the concordance. There, opposite the number 2490, we read "chalal—to bore, etc." That might give us some food for thought!

2) *The Index to Brown, Driver, Briggs Hebrew Lexicon* (Moody Press)

This is a new addition to our catalogue of Hebrew books useful to the English reader and in my opinion the best source. Unfortunately, it involves the most expense since it requires the purchase of a companion volume: *A Hebrew and English Lexicon of the Old Testament* by Brown, Driver, and Briggs (Clarendon Press: Oxford). However, these two volumes are by far the most valuable set of books you can possess for the purpose we're describing.

Let's follow the process using the same word (wounded) in Isaiah 53:5. The Index is based on the *New American Standard Bible,* so in every case we will have to determine the exact word used in that translation. If we then turn to the section of the *Index* on Isaiah 53:5 (it occurs on page 354) we would find the appropriate verb indicated by its root form, with a page number where that verb occurs in the *Lexicon* by Brown, Driver, and Briggs (p. 319b). There we would find the proper entry with the definition "bore, pierce" and the translation at Isaiah 53:5 "pierced, wounded because of our transgressions." Thus, we have arrived at the essential meaning of the term normally translated "wounded." It apparently refers to a puncture wound of some type, and so takes on added significance in view of the events of the crucifixion.

Some Final Tips

1) Italics in most translations do not indicate emphasis but omission. The italicized words do not occur in the Hebrew text but rather were added by the translators in an attempt to clarify the meanings. Try reading a text without the italicized words to get the force of the original text.

2) The personal name of God, Jehovah, or more properly, Yahweh, is normally translated "LORD," with each letter capitalized. The term of respect, "Lord," or as we would say,

"sir," is spelled "Lord" with only the first letter capitalized. The generic name for God, "Elohim," is always translated, "God." Note, for instance, the translations of Genesis 1 and 2 and the careful distinction made in the use of the names of God.

Phase 4

Structural Analysis

12

Getting It All Together

Up to now we have been majoring on the techniques of analyzing the details of the biblical text, with little attention to its structure. Now let's consider how to discern this structure and outline a passage or book.

The procedure is simple enough. We just:

1) Follow the logical progress of thought
2) Try to observe the breaks in thought
3) Put a caption or headline on each division which reflects its content.

To start out, let's try this approach on Psalm 32, just eleven verses long, so it shouldn't be too hard. It starts with the happy picture of a man who is forgiven:

> *1* Blessed is he whose transgression is forgiven,
>   whose sin is covered.
> *2* Blessed is the man to whom the Lord imputes
>   no iniquity,
>   and in whose spirit there is no deceit
>   (Ps. 32:1,2).

The next two verses talk about the misery inherent in unconfessed sin:

> *3* When I declared not my sin, my body wasted
>   away
>   through my groaning all day long.

    4 For day and night thy hand was heavy upon me;
        my strength was dried up as by the heat of
            summer (Ps. 32:3,4).

There is obvious contrast here, so we choose two contrasting captions:

Happiness is—FORGIVENESS, and
Misery is—THE BIG COVER-UP

Then we add some subheadings to reflect the content of each pair of verses, like this:

A. *Happiness is—FORGIVENESS*   vss. 1–2
    1. Transgression forgiven ⎫
                  ⎬   v. 1
    2. Sin covered ⎭
    3. Iniquity not charged ⎫
                  ⎬   v. 2
    4. A free spirit ⎭
B. *Misery is—the BIG COVER-UP*   vss. 3–4
    1. A body wasted away ⎧
                  ⎨   v. 3
    2. Continual groaning ⎩
    3. A heavy spirit ⎫
                  ⎬   v. 4
    4. No strength ⎭

At this point we read the word *Selah,* a very interesting Hebrew word found frequently in Psalms. Though the meaning is a bit obscure, it is thought to be a pause in the music (since the Psalms were sung). It apparently comes from a root word meaning *to weigh,* thus someone has said it should be translated "pause for thought," or, "just think of that!" If we consider the content of these first four verses of this Psalm, especially verse 4, we can see how it demands that we stop and think about the truth here declared.

    Reading on, we note that there is *Selah* at the end of verse 5 and also after verse 7. This gives us a clue for our next breaks in thought.

    5 I acknowledged my sin to thee,
        and I did not hide my iniquity;

I said, "I will confess my transgressions to the
  LORD";
    then thou didst forgive the guilt of my sin.

Selah

6 Therefore let every one who is godly
    offer prayer to thee;
  at a time of distress, in the rush of great waters,
    they shall not reach him.

7 Thou art a hiding place for me,
    thou preservest me from trouble;
    thou dost encompass me with deliverance. *Selah*
  (Ps. 32:5–7).

Verse 5 spells out the way to recover, so we title it, "The Way
Back," while verses 6 and 7 declare the value of this new-found
freedom. Thus we entitle it "Restored Fellowship." So now we
have, with added subpoints:

C. *The Way Back*   v. 5
   1. Admit it!
   2. God forgives!
      Think of that! (*Selah*)
D. *Restored Fellowship*   vss. 6–7
   1. Under pressure—pray.   v. 6
   2. The Lord delivers us out of our trouble—
      is our hiding place.   v. 7
      How about that? (*Selah*)

Looking ahead at the remaining four verses we see a natural
break at the end of verse 10.

8 I will instruct you and teach you
    the way you should go;
    I will counsel you with my eye upon you.
9 Be not like a horse or a mule, without understanding,
    which must be curbed with bit and bridle,
    else it will not keep with you.

10 Many are the pangs of the wicked;
     but steadfast love surrounds him who trusts in the Lord.
11 Be glad in the LORD, and rejoice, O righteous,
     and shout for joy, all you upright in heart!
     (Ps. 32:8–11).

Verses 8 through 10 tell us "How God Works" and verse 11 suggests "The Result." So we analyze the subpoints and come out like this:

E. *How God Works*   vss. 8–10
    1. By personal direction and counsel   v. 8
       a. So—don't fight it ⎱
       b. Or you'll be without it. ⎰   v. 9
    2. Crime doesn't pay—it pains ⎱
    3. Trust brings encircling love ⎰   v. 10
F. *The Result*   v. 11
    A Rejoicing Heart!

As a last step we give a title to the whole Psalm, "A Song of Forgiveness." When we put it all together it looks like this:

A SONG OF FORGIVENESS: Psalm 32

A. Happiness is—FORGIVENESS!   v.1–2
  1. Transgression forgiven. ⎱
  2. Sin covered.   v. 1
  3. Iniquity not charged. ⎱
  4. A free spirit.   v. 2
B. Misery is—the BIG COVER-UP   v. 3–4
  1. A body wasted away. ⎱
  2. Continual groaning.   v. 3
  3. A heavy spirit. ⎱
  4. No strength.   v. 4
      (Pause for thought.)
C. The Way Back   v. 5
  1. Admit it!
  2. God forgives!
      (Think of that!)

D. Restored Fellowship .... v. 6–7
   1. Under pressure—pray .... v. 6
   2. The Lord delivers—keeps us out of
      trouble—is our hiding place! .... v. 7
      (How about that?)
E. How God Works .... v. 8–10
   1. By personal direction and counsel. ...... v. 8
     a) So—don't fight it!   ⎫
     b) Or you'll be without it! ⎬ v. 9
   2. Crime doesn't pay—it pains. ⎫
   3. Trust—brings encircling love. ⎬ v. 10
F. The Result
   A REJOICING HEART! .... v. 11
     Compare 1 John 1:3–10
         Psalm 51
         Proverbs 28:13

Let's Do It Again . . .

As a final exercise let's put to work all we have been learning on a familiar but interpretively difficult passage from the New Testament—part of Romans 7 and all of Romans 8. Once again we ignore the chapter divisions, for it is not hard to see that a new chapter should *not* begin with Romans 8:1.

My first step in approaching this passage was to make my own paraphrase, simply because it is such familiar ground that I need a fresh look at it. Besides, the discipline of looking carefully at each word is exactly what I need to get me immersed in the text. Here's what I came up with, written without verse breaks to keep the flow of the thought.

7:15 Really, the way things work out in my life I do not understand, for I am not practicing what I honestly want to do, but I am doing the very thing I hate. If, then, I do what I desire not to do, I am agreeing with the law of God—that it is good. But now it is no longer I who make it work out this way, but the sin dwelling in me; for I am beginning to see that no good dwells in me, that is in my flesh, for to will is simple enough for me, but to accomplish what is good is not, for what I keep on doing is not the good things I really want to do but the evil I don't want. But if I do what I don't really desire, it is no longer I who produce this result but the sin dwelling in me.

21 I discover, then, another law: that even though I want to do good, evil is near at hand for me, for though I delight in the law of God in the inner man, yet I see a different law in my members warring against the law of my mind and taking me captive by the principle of sin being in my members.

24 Oh, me! Miserable man that I am! Who will rescue me from the body of this death? Thank God through our Lord Jesus Christ!

So, this is what I am forced to conclude: I myself with my mind am in willing slavery to the law of God, and with the flesh I am enslaved to the law of sin.

8:1 But then I remember—there is now no condemnation for those who are in Christ Jesus, for the new law of the Spirit, of life in Christ Jesus, has freed us from the law of sin and death. For what was impossible for the law of God to do, in that it was weak through the flesh, *God did* by sending his Son in the likeness of sinful man and as an offering for sin. In doing this he judged sin-in-the-flesh, cutting off its control over us, in order that the just requirement of his law might be fulfilled in us, the ones now ordering our lives not after the dictates of the flesh but in response to the spirit.

5 For there are two kinds of people, the ones whose mind is set on the flesh, and those who set their mind on the spirit. Now the mind-set which is occupied with the flesh is death, but the mind-set focused on the spirit means life and peace (because the whole mentality of the flesh is hostile to God, for it is not subject to God's law; actually it *cannot* be—and those who are in the flesh *cannot* please God). But you are not in the flesh but in the Spirit, since the Spirit of God dwells in you. And if anyone has not the Spirit of Christ he is not Christ's.

10 But if Christ is in you, two things follow: the body is dead through sin, and the Spirit is life for you because you are now right with God. And since the Spirit of him who raised Jesus from the dead dwells in you, the one who raised Christ Jesus from the dead will also impart life to your mortal bodies through his Spirit living in you. So then, brothers, we come to this momentous conclusion: *we are in no way obliged to live according to the dictates of the flesh!* Certainly if you live according to the flesh you are already in death's grip, but if by the Spirit you put to death the practices of the body you will live!

14 Now, as many as are *led* by the Spirit of God are the *sons* of God. For you did not receive a spirit of slavery to live again in fear, but you have received the Spirit of sonship by which we call God "our dear Father." This is because the Spirit himself bears witness with our spirit that we *are* the children of God, and since children, also heirs. We are heirs two ways: heirs of God, and fellow-heirs with Christ, since we suffer with him in order that we may also share the splendor of his character.

18 Actually I consider that our present sufferings are not worth comparing with the future glory to be unveiled to us. Indeed, the earnest expectation of the whole created world is eagerly anticipating the unveiling of the sons of God. In fact God's creation was subjected to futility not by its own choice, but through the one subjecting it in hope, hope that even the creation itself will be freed from its present slavery to corruption and decay into the glorious freedom of the children of God.

22 For we know that all the created world groans together and travails together until now, and not only the creation but also we ourselves, though enjoying a preview of the future through our life in the Spirit, even we groan inwardly, longing for the full experience of our sonship in the redemption of our body. Certainly in hope we were saved, but hope always looks forward to what is promised for future delivery. For what a person has in his possession why does he yet hope for? But if we hope for what we do not yet possess we wait quietly for it, patiently enduring the problems of life that surround us.

26 In the same way in which the Spirit assures us of this future glory he also supports us in our present weakness. Honestly, we do not know how to pray as we should, but the Spirit himself intercedes on our behalf with inexpressible yearnings, and the one who searches the hearts (that is, God himself) knows what is the mind of the Spirit: without saying a word he intercedes on behalf of the saints according to God's good purposes—and because of this intercession we know that God works everything together for good to those who love him, those he has called according to his purpose, because those whom he foreknew he also predetermined to be conformed to the image of his Son, that he should be the first in time and the first in rank among many brothers. And those whom he predestined thus he also called out; and those whom he called he also justified; and these he also gave the splendor of his own character.

31 What, then, can we possibly say to these things?

If God is for us (and he is) who in the world can stand against us? Indeed, he who spared not his own Son but delivered him up for us all, how will he not also, having given us him, freely give us all things?

Who can lay a single charge against God's chosen ones?

God is the one who has declared us blameless!

34 Who can condemn?

Christ Jesus, the one who died for us, but more than that is raised to be our living Lord, is at God's right hand in the place of honor and authority—and he is interceding for us!

Who can possibly separate us from the love of Christ?

Can trouble, or crisis, or persecution, or hunger, or lack of clothing, or danger, or threat of violence? As it stands on record, "For your sake we are being put to death every day; we were considered as sheep to be slaughtered." But in all these things we more than conquer through him who loved us.

38 For me it is a settled fact: I am thoroughly convinced that neither death nor life; neither mighty angels nor mighty men; neither present circumstances nor future· possibilities; not any of the powers that be; not the towering heights of God's majesty nor the depths of human degradation; no, nor any other thing in all creation can possibly separate us from the love of God given to us in Christ Jesus our Lord.

You will note that I started new paragraphs where I sensed a break in thought, but when it came to the questions at the end of chapter 8, I could not resist setting it forth in short bursts of expression simply to highlight the content in our minds. The paragraph breaks are at 7:21, 7:25, 8:5, 8:10, 8:14, 8:18, 8:26, and 8:31.

My next step was to try to put a title on each section—and an overall heading. Here's what I chose:

FROM FRUSTRATION TO FULFILLMENT
Romans 7:15 to 8:39

I. *We Have Met the Enemy and He is Us!*   7:15–8:4
   A. Our Problem, 7:15–20
   B. Our Conclusions, 7:21–25
   C. Formula for Freedom, 8:1–4

I wrestled through some interpretive problems like: what is "the flesh"? What is meant by "the sin that dwells in me"? What does "the body of this death" mean in 7:24? What is "he judged sin in the flesh" in 8:4 all about? What is "sonship" in 8:14 by contrast with being "children"? How come we have received the "Spirit of sonship" in 8:15 yet still await the full expression of sonship in 8:23? What are all the different "laws"?

You can see that I'm just full of questions—but this time I'm not going to give you any answers. This is a study book, remember? Besides, I would never think of robbing you of "the joy of discovery." This is such a crucial and rewarding scripture, I hope you are excited about pursuing its study to the satisfaction of your own heart.

I will give you my final summary outline, though. I hope it will help you think through this vital passage. *What words these are to live by!*

From Frustration to Fulfillment

2. The flesh is still around—and is incorrigibly bad. It *won't* behave! The principle of indwelling sin is what beats me!	17–20
B. *Our Conclusions*	7:21–25
1. I find the *Law of Temptation*. I can always do it wrong—even when I'm trying to do it right and agree with the law of God.	21–23
2. Is there no way out? Yes— through Jesus Christ our LORD.	25a
3. But trying to make the flesh behave through my own effort is a vain attempt.	25b
C. *Formula for Freedom*	8:1–4
1. *Really*—there's *no condemnation!*	1
2. The New Law—the law of the Spirit, of Life in *Christ Jesus*— makes all the difference.	2
3. It *frees* me from the old vicious circle of *sin and death*.	2 & 3
4. It's not my trying harder but trusting in what God *did* in Christ that sets me free.	3
5. *His Purpose*—the fulfilling of the very law that used to condemn me as I walk now in obedience to the indwelling *Spirit* —*trusting*—not *trying!*	4
II. *The Joy of Growing Up*	Romans 8:5–17
A. *Two Ways to Go*	8:5–9
1. Two options—the way of the *flesh* or the way of the *Spirit*.	5
2. Two different results—*death* or *life*.	6
3. The *flesh* is incurably hostile to God. It *cannot* behave.	7
4. Two types—those in the flesh and those in the Spirit.	8–9

B. *The Way to Maturity*	8:10–17
1. The Law of the Spirit	10–13
a. *Christ in you* makes a difference—you have resurrection life in mortal bodies.	10–11
b. So—we don't cater to the flesh, we put to death the deeds of the body—by the Spirit.	12–13
2. The Appointment to Sonship	14–17
a. The Spirit leads to mature, responsible sonship.	14
b. We're not *slaves,* but *sons, joint heirs with Christ!*	15–17
III. *Hereafter—and Here*	Romans 8:18–30
A. *Present Suffering and Future Glory*	18–26a
1. No comparison	18
2. Real contrast	19–26a

Now	*Then*
Suffering	Glory
Waiting	Revealing
Eager longing	Creation set free
Futility	Glorious liberty
Hope	Our full inheritance—
Bondage to	(son-placing)
decay	Redeemed bodies
Groaning in	
travail	
Down payment	
(the Spirit)	
Patient waiting	
Weakness	

B. *Adequate Resources and Ultimate Aim*	Romans 8:26b–30
1. The Spirit's intercession—knowing what I need	26–27
2. The resulting experience—all for my good	28
3. The final goal—conformed to His image	29

The Last Word

There are some who become so preoccupied with textual criticism that they never seem to get to the text of scripture. And though most of us are not likely to get caught in that trap, there is a similar danger we must be alert to avoid. It is this: we can become so involved in the detail of Bible study and interpretation that we may miss the point of it all. The point is that we may know, in living reality, the One upon whom it focuses, the Lord Jesus Christ. If we miss him, in all the unsurpassed value of his work for us and in us, we are only engaging in pointless exegetical exercise.

In some ways, the current tempest revolving around the question of biblical inerrancy can assume the same significance, and I wonder if we are not trying to catch a straw in the wind. It is possible for us to make the Bible the battleground of our orthodoxy and be unspiritual in the process. All of us know people who "believe the Bible from cover to cover," but whose lives show little evidence of a living relationship with the Lord it seeks to present.

And lest I be misunderstood, I personally have no doubt about the Bible's inerrancy. But that doctrinal assertion does not make me Christlike. For no matter with what passionate conviction we hold to the utter trustworthiness of the Bible and contend for its inerrancy, we need to recognize that it is only an instrument in the hands of God (although an immensely valuable one) to bring us to the fullness of life in Christ. It is the incorruptible seed through which we experience new birth; it is the mirror which shows us what we are really like; it is the sword of the Spirit by which the enemy of our souls may be defeated; it is the lamp which lights our pathway through life—and much more. But all of this only because it relates us in love, and in power, to the One who has made us his inheritance.

No wonder, then, the apostle prays:

. . . that the God of our Lord Jesus Christ, the Father of glory, may give you a spirit of wisdom and of revelation in the knowledge of him, having the eyes of your hearts enlightened, that you may know

1) what is the hope to which he has called you,
2) what are the riches of his glorious inheritance in the saints, and

3) what is the immeasurable greatness of his power in us
who believe according to the working of his great might
which he accomplished in Christ when he raised him
from the dead and made him . . . far above all rule and
authority and dominion . . . and put all things under his
feet, and has made him head over all things for the
church, which is his body . . . (Eph. 1:17–22).

How thankful we should be for the objective revelation,
the Word of God, and the subjective illuminating ministry
of the Spirit of God—both dedicated to the same end, to
make the Lord Jesus a living reality in our lives!

That's why God has given us his words to *live* by.

Index to the Appendix

Basic Grammatical Data

A. *Parts of Speech*—Communication through language utilizes *words* which have been assigned certain functions. This gives us the various types of words which we call the parts of speech.

Noun: names a person, place or thing, e.g. *apostle, city, book.*

Verb: describes action regarding noun, e.g. *read, rejoice, write.*

Adjective: describes, limits or qualifies noun, e.g. *faithful, great.*

Pronoun: used instead of noun, e.g. *I, you, he, she, they, it.*

Adverb: describes, limits or qualifies verb, e.g. *truly, quickly.*

Preposition: placed before a noun to relate to other words, e.g. *in, to, for, beside, among, with, by.*

Conjunction: joins together words, phrases, clauses, e.g. *and, but.*

These parts of speech are joined together to make a:

Sentence: a group of words expressing a complete thought.

Phrase: a grammatical unit without subject or verb, modifying the sense or the main thought of a clause or sentence.

Clause: consisting of a subject and a predicate expressing the main thought or a dependent or subordinate thought. (More detail on phrases and clauses follows)

Paragraph: containing a block of thought related to one theme.

B. *Nouns have Case*—(rather a lost feature of English, but not in foreign languages)

Nominative: the subject, e.g. *Abraham* believed God.

Genitive: possession or description, e.g. the gospel *of God.*

Dative: indirect object, e.g. preach the gospel *to the Gentiles.*

Accusative: direct object, e.g. send *Timothy.*

C. *Verbs have:*

Person: 1st, 2nd, or 3rd, e.g. *I say, you say, he says.*

Number: Singular or plural, e.g. *I say, we say.*

Tense: time relationships

   a. *Present* . . . I go (or I am going)

   b. *Past* . . . I went

   c. *Future* . . . I shall go

   d. *Present Perfect* . . . I have gone

   e. *Past Perfect* . . . I had gone

f. *Future Perfect* . . . I shall have gone

Voice: relationship of action to subject

   a. *Active* (The subject does the acting) e.g. *Timothy taught*

   b. *Passive* (The subject is acted upon) e.g. *Timothy was taught*

Mood: reflecting the attitude of the one acting or speaking

   a. *Indicative* (the mood of declaration) e.g. *I will come* again.

   b. *Imperative* (the mood of command) e.g. *Rejoice* always.

   c. *Subjunctive* (the mood of contingency used in conditional clauses, exhortations, and where the outcome is in doubt.) This is almost a lost feature of English, but important in New Testament Greek, e.g. *let us go on* to maturity.

There are auxiliary verb forms like *Participles* (verbal adjectives modifying the thought or action of the main verb). They participate in the action, e.g. *going*, make disciples . . . *teaching* them.

D. *Consider Clauses*

1. There is the *main clause*, which is a clause that can stand alone and express a complete thought by itself.

2. There are *modifying clauses* which are subordinate to the main clause and are used to modify, describe or limit the thought of the main clause. Clauses express various forms of modifying thought:

   a. CAUSE—*because, since,* e.g. Matt. 25:40, John 14:19

   b. COMPARISON—*as, even as, just as, even so, than,* e.g. 1 Cor. 4:1, Heb. 4:2, Matt. 23:27, Heb. 1:4

   c. LOCATION—*where, whence,* e.g. Mark 4:5, Matt. 12:44

   d. TIME—*before, when, until, while, whenever,* e.g. Matt. 19:1, Mark 11:25, John 14:29

   e. PURPOSE—*that, in order that, that not, lest* (*aim* of the action of the verb) e.g. John 1:7, Matt 7:1, 2 Cor. 1:16, Matt. 6:5

   f. RESULT—*so, so that, so as to* (*consequence* of the action of the verb) e.g. 1 Cor. 13:2, Mark 1:27, Rom. 15:9 & 7:3

   g. EXPLANATION OR CONCLUSION—*for, therefore, wherefore, nevertheless,* e.g. 2 Pet. 2:4, Phil. 2:9, Rom. 8:1, Heb. 12:1

    h. CONDITION—*if,* e.g. Gal. 5:18, John 1:9

E. *Notice Prepositional Phrases*—Prepositions are generally little words, but they are not without great significance. They express many shades of thought:

1. *Direction—up, from, through, out of, into, unto, to, up to, along, down, upon, throughout, beyond, from, around, about, toward.*
2. *Position—in, by, on, at, among, within, upon, before, over, from, beside, under.*
3. *Relation—instead of, for, besides, as, for, against, in respect to, after, in the time of, according to, with reference to, after, contrary to, in behalf of, concerning, about, pertaining to.*
4. *Agency—by, in.*
5. *Means—through, by means of, with*
6. *Cause—because of, on account of*
7. *Association—with*
8. *Purpose—for the sake of, for the purpose of, for.*

Structural Relationships—Also, in our study, it is well to observe some of the other features of language:

1. Look for repeated words, phrases, and ideas which may be a clue to the important thoughts the author had in mind. For example, count the "much more's" in Romans 5.
2. Find relationships between units of expression based on contrast, comparison, repetition, or cause and effect. Look for *purpose* clauses, usually headed by the words "that," or "in order that." Look for *result* clauses, usually begun by "so" or "so that" or "in order to."

    Here's a pointed example of purpose clauses expressing the *aim* of the action.

. . . *always carrying about in the body the death* (or better, dying) *of Jesus,* so that *the life of Jesus may also be manifested in our bodies. For while we live we are always being given up to death for Jesus' sake,* so that *the life of Jesus may be manifested in our mortal flesh* (2 Cor. 4:10,11).

The twice-repeated *so that the life of Jesus may be manifested in our bodies* is clearly the purpose God intends for us.

For more detailed information on grammar consult Braun *English Grammar for Language Students,* distributed by Ulrick's Books, Inc., 549 East University Avenue, Ann Arbor, Michigan 48104.

Bibliography

1. Books Mentioned in the Text

Stuart Briscoe, *All Things Weird and Wonderful* (Wheaton: Victor Books, 1977).

Brown, Driver, and Briggs, *A Hebrew and English Lexicon of the Old Testament* (New York: Oxford University Press, n.d.).

Eimspahr, *Index to Brown, Driver, and Briggs Lexicon* (Chicago: Moody Press, n.d.).

E. W. Bullinger, *Figures of Speech Used in the Bible* (Grand Rapids: Baker Book House, 1968).

Alfred Edersheim, *The Life and Times of Jesus the Messiah* (Grand Rapids: Wm. B. Eerdmans, 1962).

Orville J. Nave and S. Maxwell Coder, *Nave's Topical Bible* (Chicago: Moody Press, 1975).

Aaron Pick, *Dictionary of Old Testament Words for English Readers* (Grand Rapids: Kregel Publications, n.d.).

James Strong, *Strong's Exhaustive Concordance of the Bible* (Waco: Word Books, 1977).

Ray Stedman, *The Queen and I* (Waco: Word Books, 1978).

Milton S. Terry, *Biblical Hermeneutics* (Grand Rapids: Zondervan, n.d.).

Thompson's Chain Reference Bible (Indianapolis: B. B. Kirkbride Bible Company, 1934).

R. E. Trench, *Notes on the Miracles and Parables of Our Lord* (Old Tappan, N.J.: Fleming H. Revell Co., 1953).

Merrill F. Unger, *Unger's Bible Dictionary* (Chicago: Moody Press, 1957).

W. E. Vine, *Expository Dictionary of New Testament Words* (Old Tappan, N.J.: Fleming H. Revell Co., 1962).

Oletta Wald, *The Joy of Discovery in Bible Study* (Minneapolis: Augsburg, 1975).

Fred H. Wight, *Manners and Customs of Bible Lands* (Chicago: Moody Press, 1953).

A Layman's Guide to Bible Versions and Bible Enjoyment (Philadelphia: Eternity Magazine, 1974).

2. Basic Exegetical Study Books

Yohanan Aharoni and Michael Avi-Yonah, *Macmillan Bible Atlas* (New York: Macmillan, 1965).

J. D. Douglas, *The New Bible Dictionary* (Grand Rapids: Wm. B. Eerdmans, 1962).

G. T. Manley, *The New Bible Handbook* (London: The Inter-Varsity Fellowship, n.d.).

James Strong, *Strong's Exhaustive Concordance* of the Bible (Waco: Word, 1977).

Merrill F. Unger, *Unger's Bible Dictionary* (Chicago: Moody Press, 1957).

A good Dictionary of the English language.

3. *Greek Study Books for the English Reader*

Alfred Marshall, *The Interlinear Greek-English New Testament* (London: Samuel Bagster and Sons, Ltd., 1959).

Archibald T. Robertson, *Word Pictures in the New Testament* (New York: Harper and Row, 1952).

W. E. Vine, *Expository Dictionary of New Testament Words* (Old Tappan, N.J., 1962).

Kenneth S. Wuest, *The Practical Use of the Greek New Testament* (Chicago: Moody Press, 1946).

Kenneth S. Wuest, *Word Studies from the Greek New Testament for English Readers* (Grand Rapids: Wm. B. Eerdmans).

4. *Greek Study Books for the Greek Reader*

Analytical Greek Lexicon (London: Bagster, n.d.)

W. F. Arndt and F. W. Gingrich, *A Greek-English Lexicon of the New Testament* (Grand Rapids: Zondervan, n.d.).

H. E. Dana and J. R. Mantey, *Manual Grammar of the Greek New Testament* (New York: Macmillan, 1960).

Englishman's Greek Concordance (London: Bagster, 1903).

E. S. Han, *A Parsing Guide to the Greek New Testament* (Scottdale, Pa.: Herald Press, 1971).

Gerhard Kittel and Gerhard Friedrich, *Theological Dictionary of the New Testament* (Grand Rapids: Wm. B. Eerdmans, 1974) nine volumes.

William S. LaSor, *Handbook of New Testament Greek* (Grand Rapids: Wm. B. Eerdmans, 1973).

W. Robertson Nicoll, *The Expositor's Greek New Testament* (Grand Rapids: Wm. B. Eerdmans, 1961) five volumes.

Joseph H. Thayer, *Greek-English Lexicon of the New Testament* (New York: American Book Co., 1889).

Robert C. Trench, *Synonyms of the New Testament* (Grand Rapids: Wm. B. Eerdmans, 1960).

5. *Hebrew Helps for the English Reader*

G. Johannes Botterweck and Helmer Ringgren, *Theological Dictionary of the Old Testament* (Grand Rapids: Wm. B. Eerdmans, 1975).

Brown, Driver, and Briggs, *A Hebrew and English Lexicon of the Old Testament* (London: Oxford University Press, n.d.).

Eimspahr, *Index to Brown, Driver, and Briggs Hebrew Lexicon* (Chicago: Moody Press, n.d.).

Carl F. Keil and Franz Delitszch, *Commentary on the Old Testament* (Grand Rapids: Wm. B. Eerdmans, n.d.) ten volumes.

Aaron Pick, *Dictionary of Old Testament Words for English Readers* (Grand Rapids: Kregel Publications, n.d.).

6. *Biblical Introductions and New Testament Harmonies*

Donald Guthrie, *The New Bible Commentary* (Grand Rapids: Wm. B. Eerdmans, 1970).

Roland K. Harrison, *Introduction to the Old Testament* (Grand Rapids: Wm. B. Eerdmans, 1969).

Archibald T. Robertson, *Harmony of the Gospels* (New York: Harper and Rowe, 1922).

Merrill C. Tenney, *New Testament Survey* (Grand Rapids: Wm. B. Eerdmans, 1961).

7. *Helps on Figurative Language*

E. W. Bullinger, *Figures of Speech Used in the Bible* (Grand Rapids: Baker Book House, 1968).

G. Campbell Morgan, *Parables and Metaphors of Our Lord* (Old Tappan, N.J.: Fleming H. Revell Co., 1943).

R. E. Trench, *Notes on the Miracles and Parables of Our Lord* (Old Tappan, N.J., Fleming H. Revell Co., 1953).

Walter L. Wilson, *Dictionary of Bible Types* (Grand Rapids: Wm. B. Eerdmans, 1957).

8. Helps on Historical and Cultural Backgrounds

David and Patricia Alexander, *Eerdmans' Handbook to the Bible* (Grand Rapids: Wm. B. Eerdmans, 1973).

William Barclay, *Daily Bible Study* series (Philadelphia: Westminster Press, 1960). This series is good on backgrounds but inadequate theologically.

F. F. Bruce, *New Testament History* (New York: Doubleday and Co., 1972).

Alfred Edersheim, *Sketches of Jewish Social Life* (Grand Rapids: Wm. B. Eerdmans, 1974).

Everyday Life in Bible Times (Washington, D.C.: National Geographic Society, 1967).

Roland K. Harrison, *Old Testament Times* (Grand Rapids: Wm. B. Eerdmans, 1969).

Bruce M. Metzger, *The New Testament: Its Background, Growth, and Content* (New York: Abingdon Cokesbury Press, 1965).

Merrill C. Tenney, *The New Testament Times* (Grand Rapids: Wm. B. Eerdmans, 1965).

Merrill F. Unger, *Archeology and the New Testament* (Grand Rapids: Zondervan Publishing House, 1962).

Merrill F. Unger, *Archeology and the Old Testament* (Grand Rapids: Zondervan Publishing House, 1954).

Howard F. Vos and Charles P. Pfeiffer, *Wycliffe Historical Geography of Bible Lands* (Chicago: Moody Press, 1967).

9. General Reference Works

James Orr, *The International Standard Bible Encyclopedia* (Grand Rapids: Wm. B. Eerdmans, 1930). Five volumes.

Merrill C. Tenney, *The Zondervan Pictorial Encyclopedia of the Bible* (Grand Rapids: Zondervan Publishing House, 1975). Five volumes.

10. Commentaries

It is suggested that the most advantageous way to use commentaries is to seek out the best book you can find at your Christian bookstore on the individual book of the Bible you are studying, using it *after* you have done your own exegetical study. Then the next time you study or teach that Bible book choose another commentary to augment your own study. This will give you a different author's slant each time you study, and build your library in the process. For example, I used Newell's *Romans Verse by Verse* (Moody) the first time I studied Romans and found it invaluable. But the next time I studied Romans I used Stifler's *The Epistle to the Romans* (Moody). The next time through I used Barnhouse's four volume study of Romans, *Exposition of Bible Doctrines* (Eerdmans).

Each time I did my own independent study, then checked the commentators to see what they had discovered that I had missed. This procedure gives God the first opportunity to instruct my mind and heart, without a human intermediary.

Appendix C

Study Questions on 2 Timothy
by
David H. Roper

Introductory Background Study

Read 2 Timothy through twice.
1. What were Paul's circumstances? (Note particularly 4:9–18)
2. What bearing does Paul's situation have on his reason for writing this letter?
3. What can you discern about Timothy's personality from reading this letter?
4. Where was he at the time the letter was written? (There is a clue in the letter).
   For additional information on Paul's relationship to Timothy read Acts 16:1–5 and use a concordance to note other passages where Timothy is linked to Paul.
5. What further conclusions can you draw about Timothy?
6. Now look up the entries for Paul and Timothy in a Bible dictionary. What additional facts have you uncovered that you may have overlooked before?

Chapter One

Read Chapter 1 (5–10 times).
1. What are the paragraph divisions in your Bible? Do you agree that the chapter should be divided in this manner? How would you divide the chapter?
2. Verses 1 and 2 are obviously the salutation or introduction to the letter. Salutations to correspondence of the first century generally followed this pattern "A (writer) to B (recipient) greeting." What elements does Paul add that are distinctively Christian? What do these additions tell us about the apostle's ministry?
3. Define (a) Grace (b) Mercy (c) Peace (Use a Bible or English Dictionary). How do they differ?
4. *Verses 3–5* contain Paul's word of thanksgiving to God for his friendship with Timothy. What aspects of that relationship caused Paul to give thanks?
5. *Read 6–14* again. Note the imperatives (commands). Underscore them in your Bible. The argument in this section revolves around these verbs.
   6–14 begins with the clause, "And for this reason . . ." For what reason? This "reason" is evidently the basis of the commands

that follow. What does this fact tell us about the nature of obedience?

6. The first command "kindle afresh" is found in verse 6. What fundamental fact does that metaphor suggest?

7. The "gift of God" referred to in verse 6 is either a *spiritual gift* (i.e. a divinely given capacity for service, cf. Cor. 12:4–11; Rom. 12:3–8) or the gift of the *Holy Spirit*. Which do you think it is? Why? (Use a concordance to see how Paul uses this term. Observe especially the occurrence of this word in the first letter to Timothy. Note also the context of this verse, especially verse 7.)

8. *Verse 7* begins with the conjunction "for" indicating that the information in this verse explains the action in verse 6. For what reason then is Timothy to *kindle afresh the gift of God?*

9. What is the tense of the verb "has (not) given"? What does this tense indicate about the nature of the gift?

10. Define (1) Power (2) Love (3) Discipline (dictionary).

11. The second imperative is found in verse 8. It is stated both negatively ("do not be ashamed") and positively ("join with me in suffering"). Of what was Timothy tempted to be ashamed? Why? (Observe carefully!)

12. *Verse 8* begins with another conjunction "Therefore . . ." indicating the verse states a logical conclusion to the preceding argument. What is the force then of Paul's command? On what basis is Timothy to unashamedly join with Paul in suffering?

13. What relationship does the section *9–11* have to the development of Paul's argument? (At first these verses seem to be disconnected but *look again!*) Note the phrase "I also suffer . . . I am not ashamed." Compare with verse 8. This entire section from 8–12 appears to be one unit of thought dealing with shame and suffering, does it not? How does it fit together logically? (Note the occurrence of the term "gospel" in this section. Repeated words or ideas sometimes give you the key to understanding a passage.)

14. What are the elements of the gospel as Paul enumerates them in verses 9 and 10?

15. *Verse 12* can be translated in two different ways:
    (1) RSV "He is able to guard until that day *what has been entrusted to me.*"
    (2) ASV "He is able to guard *what I have entrusted to Him* until that day."
    Both translations are legitimate. The Greek states ambiguously "He is able to guard *my commitment* until that day."
    What is the essential difference in the two translations cited above?

16. What is it that is "entrusted"? Which translation do you consider accurate? Read carefully the immediate context (8–14).

17. The third command is found in *verse 13:* "Retain the standard

of sound words." Compare this translation with other versions. What are the "sound words" to which he refers? Is there something in the context that will help you understand that phrase?

18. How do you "retain . . . sound words, . . . *in the faith and love* which are in Christ Jesus"? What is the meaning of this verse in practical terms?

19. The fourth and final command is found in *verse 15,* "Guard . . . the treasure." What is the treasure that has been entrusted to Timothy? (Again pay particular attention to the context.)

20. Compare verse 14 with verse 12. What do verses 12 and 14 teach about the nature of human activity? (cp. Phil. 2:13, 14)

21. Does verse 14 help you in interpreting the nature of the "gift" in verse 6?

22. Verses 15–18 are a new paragraph. What is the subject of this section?

23. What is the relationship of this paragraph to the one preceding (3–14)?

24. What verb found in verses 15–18 is repeated twice in the paragraph 3–14?

25. Who is the subject of the verb in each case?

26. Does this help you to see the relationship of these two paragraphs?

27. What is the region referred to as "Asia" in verse 15? (Refer to a Bible dictionary.)

28. What churches were located there?

29. Why is it significant that "all" had turned away from Paul in Asia?

30. What further information does that give us about Timothy's situation? Compare 2 Timothy 4:16.

31. Who was Onesiphorus? (His name occurs in the New Testament only here and 4:19.)

32. Read the paragraph again for clues to his condition at the time Paul wrote this letter.

33. What do you think happened to him? Why?

34. Now think again! What part does the information contained in verses 15–18 play in Paul's word of encouragement to Timothy?

Chapter Two

Read chapter 2 (5–10 times.)

1. The New American Standard Bible divides the chapter into two paragraphs; *1–13* and *14–26.* Do you think this arrangement is valid?

2. Observe the main verbs in chapter 2. You will note again, as in chapter 1, that most of them are commands. Mark the imperatives in your Bible in some conspicuous way.

3. Note that the second word in *verse 1* is the conjunction "therefore." Remember that this term introduces a conclusion or inference (cp. 1:8). The action of the verb is based on some prior fact. On what basis, then, is Timothy to be strong?

4. What further incentive to "be strong" is contained in the verse itself?

5. Why are these two incentives so important in Timothy's case?

6. *Verse 2* also begins with a conjunction, "and." What does this connective suggest concerning the action of the two commands in verses one and two?

7. Recall Timothy's nature. What was he naturally inclined to do?

8. How many generations are envisioned in verse 2?

9. What pattern of ministry is established in this verse?

10. What characteristic is Timothy to look for in those to whom he is ministering?

11. Assuming that you "entrust" the truth to one faithful individual each year and equip that person to reach one more each succeeding year and the process continues unbroken for twenty years how many will be reached?

12. The second command in this chapter is found in *verse 3*, "suffer hardship with me." Read 2:3–13 again. How does Paul develop his argument? Are there any repeated words or ideas that indicate the theme of these verses?

13. Again, what does this teaching suggest about Timothy's natural inclination toward his assignment in Ephesus?

14. Paul uses three illustrative metaphors in this section. What are they and what specific attribute does each one illustrate?

15. Note that in each case there is a responsibility and a reward. What are they?

16. *Verse 7* contains a command and a promise that ought to encourage you on in your study!

17. *Verse 8* contains another command *"Remember* Jesus Christ." Why does he insert this statement at this point in the argument?

18. Note the order of the Lord's names. Is this Paul's normal order in this book?

19. (Use a concordance and note occurrences of the names or quickly re-read 2 Timothy.) What does this order suggest about the Lord that would encourage Timothy?

20. What does the designation "descendant of David" add to the argument? Why not "Son of God"?

21. Why is it important to Timothy that he is "risen from the dead"?

22. *In verse 9* Paul refers again to his own circumstances. He is imprisoned but the word of God is not, what does he mean?

23. What effect would that statement have on Timothy?

24. According to *verse 10,* Paul's reason for enduring all things is twofold. The phrase "for this reason" looks back to some fact in verse 10. What is it?

25. The "that" in verse 10 introduces a *purpose clause* (a purpose clause expresses the aim of the action indicated by the main verb), and supplies a second reason for endurance. What is it?

26. Paul is quoting a portion of an ancient hymn or early liturgical formula in *verses 11–13.* It is designated "a trustworthy statement" or a word to be believed. How does this hymn develop Paul's argument? What new facts pertaining to suffering hardship are introduced?

27. What incentives and warnings would Timothy receive?

28. And what about us?

29. Note the problem in *verses 12 and 13.* What is the difference between denying him and proving faithless? (The consequences certainly differ!)

30. The second paragraph in this chapter begins with *verse 14.* Read verses 14–26 again. What is the theme of this division?

31. How does it differ from 2:1–13?

32. To whom is the reminder and solemn charge in verse 14 addressed (cp. 2:2)?

33. In this paragraph Paul is contrasting two classes of workmen. What are the methods of each class and the results that their methods produce?

34. The crux of this paragraph is *verse 15.* The approved workman who has no need to be ashamed *handles the word of truth accurately.* What does that phrase mean? Compare various translations. The Greek actually says "(he) cuts straight to the goal."

35. What is the goal of all biblical instruction? Cp. 2:25; 3:16; 1 Timothy 1:5.

36. Contrast this goal with the results of the disapproved workmen whose methods Paul condemns.

37. Note *verse 19.* The conjunction "nevertheless" denotes *contrast.* Paul is contrasting two truths: one found in verse 18, the other in verse 19. What is Paul contrasting?

38. Why would verse 19 particularly encourage Timothy?

39. In verse 19 what two seemingly contradictory principles comprise God's "seal"?

40. To what do the vessels of honor and dishonor correspond in *verse 20?* (Remember the context!)

41. Note that the New American Standard Bible has placed the word "things" in italics (in *verse 21*). Most versions use italics to indicate words that are *added* in the translation to clarify but do not occur in the original language. In this passage the translators want you to know that the pronoun "these" does not refer to the

vessels but to something else. Do you agree with their thinking?

42. From what, then, is Timothy to cleanse himself?
43. *Verse 22* contains a command to "flee youthful lusts." In English the term lusts almost always refers to sexual matters. The Greek term, however, from which this word is translated means "desires" and is a much broader term referring to almost any sort of strong passion. Now, noting again the context, what are the strong passions that might drive and control young Timothy?
44. What pursuits would serve Timothy better?
45. Define righteousness, faith, love and peace.
46. Are these attributes that Timothy himself should possess or a climate that he should seek in the church?
47. *Verse 23* is in contrast with verse 22 ("But"). Does this help you answer the last question?
48. *Verses 24–26* provide a look behind the scenes. Why do people oppose the gospel?
49. Who then is the enemy?
50. Does this truth affect your attitude toward those who are in opposition to you?
51. What are the characteristics of God's bondservant?

That's two chapters—now you do the rest!

[This material is used by permission of the author and publisher and may be purchased in its entirety under the title *Heart to Know the Word,* Roper Press, Dallas, Texas.]

Sample Outlines

A Song about Man
Psalm 53

A. *The Problem Posed*	v. 1
the folly of godlessness	
B. *God's Appraisal*	v. 2&3
1. He sees	v. 2
2. He judges	v. 3
C. *God's Question*	v. 4
Have they no understanding?	
D. *Man's End—without God*	v. 5
terror,	
death,	
shame,	
rejection.	
E. *Man's Need*	v. 6
deliverance,	
restoration,	
rejoicing!	

Compare Psalms 14 and 12, Romans 3:9–18

A Song of Victory
Psalm 60

A. *The Desolation of Defeat*	v. 1–4
1. A sense of rejection by God.	v. 1
2. Broken defenses.	
3. Insecure footing.	v. 2
4. Suffering hard things.	
5. Bewilderment.	v. 3
B. But—*A Plea for Help*	
Restore us.	v. 1
Repair the breaches.	v. 2
C. *A Ray of Hope*	v. 4–5
1. A rallying point—a banner	v. 4
(THINK ABOUT IT!)	
2. A place of deliverance and victory.	v. 5
D. *God's Word on the Subject*	v. 6–8
1. Widespread victory declared.	v. 6–7
2. Humiliation of the enemy is sure.	v. 8
E. *But How Can It Be?*	v. 9–12
1. The enemy forces are imposing.	v. 9

2. If God is not with us—we're sunk!   v. 10
3. A PRAYER of DEPENDENCE—that does it!   v. 11
4. *If God Be for Us—Who Can Stand Against Us?*   v. 12
Compare: Rom. 8:31–39; 2 Cor. 2:14, 3:4–6, 4:7–12, 6:1–10

A Song of Confidence
Psalm 62

A. *The Ground of Confidence*   v. 1&2
   1. Salvation from God   v. 1
   2. His character—my rock, my fortress   v. 2
   3. The result—stability, safety   v. 2
B. *The Need for Confidence*   v. 3, 4
   1. The character of man—destructive, unfriendly,
      lying, deceitful
      (THINK OF THAT!)
C. *The Source of Hope*   v. 5–8
   1. The SAME GOD of strength and help.   v. 5
   2. My expectation is from Him.   v. 5
   3. So—I remain unshaken   v. 6
   4. In Him—safety and security—I'm with Him!   v. 7
   5. How 'bout you?   v. 8
      (THINK ABOUT IT!)
D. *A False Hope—Man*   v. 9, 10
   1. Have you ever weighed your breath?   v. 9
   2. Or counted your money?   v. 10
E. *The Final Word*   v. 11, 12
   1. POWER BELONGS TO GOD!   v. 11
   2. AND STEADFAST LOVE!   v. 12

*How do you operate
in the light
of this?*

See 2 Cor. 5:9, 10—also 1 Cor. 1:23–25; Rom. 1:16; 2 Tim. 1:7;
   1 John 4:16–18

A Song of Consolation
Psalm 73

A. *A Statement of Fact*   v. 1
   God is good to the upright!

B. *The Temptation Confronted*   v. 2–14
    Envy of the ungodly.   v. 2, 3
    1. Their apparent prosperity   v. 4–12
    2. My pointless purity.   v. 13, 14
       A clean heart and innocent hands don't pay!
C. *The Real Truth*   v. 15–20
    1. Learned in the sanctuary of God.   v. 17
       a. Where I see their end—slippery places, destroyed, swept away by terrors—a nightmare!   v. 18–20
D. *True Value Declared*   v. 21–28
    1. I was stupid to think that way.   v. 21, 22
    2. Even when my thoughts are wrong—
       I'm with you!   v. 23
       a. You hold my hand.   v. 23
       b. You guide me with your counsel. ⎫
       c. You will receive me into glory. ⎬ v. 24
       d. I have you—in heaven.   ⎫
       e. You're all I need on earth.   ⎬ v. 25
       f. I'm physically failing, but eternally secure in God.   v. 26
       g. I'm not in the place of those who perish.   v. 27
       h. My portion—*to be near God*— my strength and refuge.   v. 28
That's why I tell about all He does for me!

Secret of a Thankful Heart

Psalm 116

A. The *Reason* for LOVE   v. 1–4
    The redeeming grace of God, Who literally
      "saves our life."
B. The *Source* of LOVE   v. 5, 6
    A God Who is: GRACIOUS
                    RIGHTEOUS
                    MERCIFUL
    to keep the simple—
    save the ones brought low.
C. The *Result* of LOVE   v. 7–9
    1. Rest   v. 7, 8
    2. A godly walk, abundant life.   v. 9

D. The *Response* of LOVE   v. 10–19
  1. Keeping the faith.   v. 10, 11
  2. Taking the cup of salvation.   v. 12, 13
  3. Paying our vows.   v. 14&18
    a. Showing forth life out of death   v. 15, 16
  4. Offering sacrifices of thanksgiving   v. 17
  5. Praising the Lord before everyone   v. 19

The Prayer of Jehoshaphat
2 Chronicles 20:1–23

I. *Background*   2 Chron.
  A. The unholy alliance with Ahab.   18:1–3
  B. The crushing defeat at Ramoth-gilead.
    The mighty army of Judah defeated—
    Jehoshaphat escapes with his life   18:30–34
  C. Jehoshaphat's rebuke by Jehu, his repentance   19:1–3
    and reforms.   19:4–7
  D. Moab and Ammon attack.   20:1, 2
II. *Jehoshaphat's Prayer*
2 Chron. 20:3–13
  A. Elements of the prayer
    1. God's sovereignty over all nations   v. 6
    2. God's purpose—to give Israel the land.   v. 7, 8
    3. God's promise to answer their plea for
     help.   v. 9
    4. God's previous work to spare these
     enemies.   v. 10
    5. The present dire emergency (Deut. 2:4–
     9) and their helplessness before the enemy. v. 11, 12
     We have no might—our eyes are upon
     thee!
    6. The unity of their plea.   v. 13
III. *God's Answer*
  A. Be not afraid or dismayed—*the battle is not*
    yours but God's.   v. 15
  B. *They believed the word of God!*
IV. *The Result*
  A. Worship and praise.   20:18–22
  B. The enemy destroyed himself.   20:23, 24
  C. Beracah (blessing).   v. 26
V. *The keynote of Jehoshaphat's prayer—Reliance*
  upon God ALONE!

Not friends, counselors, alliances, churches, pastors—all are but "broken reeds" alongside the *ALL SUFFICIENT LORD.*

We have no might—our eyes are on thee!   20:12
Be not afraid—the battle is the Lord's!   20:15
                               and 17

Jehoshaphat (Jehovah judges)

2 Chronicles 20

A. *Principles of Prayer*
Remember—
1) God's sovereignty.
2) God's purposes.
3) God's promise.
4) Our helplessness.
5) Our interdependence.
6) It's God's battle—already won!
7) His *present* word to us.
8) Our place—*Reliance on God Alone! Genuine Faith!*

B. *Typology here:*
Who are the enemy forces?
Moab, Ammon, Edomites. All descendants of Esau— *Esau pictures the flesh.*
God left these people in close proximity to Israel—just as we are constantly confronted with the flesh.

C. *How do we deal with the flesh?*
1) Remember the victory of the Cross (Rom. 6:6).
2) Pray—by *faith* claim the victory God promises.
3) Worship—praise the Lord even before the victory is seen.

D. *Real Reliance—Dependence Born of Desperation!*
1) We are POWERLESS—but our eyes are on thee!
2) FEAR NOT—for the battle is not yours but God's!
3) You will not need to fight—stand still and see the victory of the Lord on your behalf!

Brief Summary of Hebrews

I. *The Superiority of the Person of Christ*
Chapter 1. His deity declared
Chapter 2. His humanity declared
A. Christ greater than prophets   1:1–3

B. Christ greater than angels   1:4–2:18
C. Christ greater than Moses   3:1–19
D. Christ greater than Joshua   4:1–16

    Consider Him . . .   3:1
He is LORD
    GOD
    CREATOR
    REDEEMER
Therefore—
1. Don't *neglect* so *great salvation!*
2. Don't *disbelieve*—and thus fail to enter into His *rest.*
3. Be intensely earnest to enter into His Rest—for
    a) the Word of God reveals our need to our hearts.
    b) God knows all about us—we cannot hide.
    c) We come to a throne of *grace.*

II. *The Superiority of the Priesthood of Christ*   4:14–10:18
   A. *Christ greater than Aaron*   5:1–10:18
   Aaron was sinful—Christ is sinless.
   Aaronic priests were many—Christ is one.
   They died—He lives forever.
   They offered animals—He gave *Himself.*
   Christ is the priest of:
      A BETTER COVENANT
      A BETTER TABERNACLE
      A BETTER SACRIFICE
   Because He is the *reality* of which the shadow speaks!
   The fulfillment of all the types and pictures.
   The Appeal
   God who spoke in times past—by the prophets—has now spoken . . .
      IN HIS SON
   See that you refuse not *Him who speaks!*
   Don't go back to the old regime—the *Law.*
   It points to *Christ, our great high priest*—

at once the perfect *priest* and the perfect *sacrifice—Who is able to perfect completely those who come to God by Him.*

III. *The Superiority of Life in Christ*   10:19–13:25

  A. Gives boldness, access, nearness, a *love* relationship, union with Christ as members of His Body   10:19–39

  B. Is a *Faith* relationship with Jesus Christ as the object of faith—the *Pioneer/Finisher* of our faith.   11:1–12:2

  C. Calls us to Mt. Zion (a place of kingship) not to Mt. Sinai (a place of awesome fear). Calls us to God, and to Jesus, the Mediator of the *new* covenant.   12:3–29

  D. Calls us to a new ALTAR—not the brazen altar of the Temple, but the *cross,* where the *perfect High Priest* made the *perfect sacrifice—Himself.*   13:1–12

  E. *The Result*—The God of peace, who brought again from the dead our Lord Jesus, that *Great Shepherd* of the sheep, through the blood of an *eternal* covenant, aims to fully qualify you in every good thing to accomplish *His will,* to do in us that which is well pleasing in His sight, through Jesus Christ, our Lord.

Chapter Headings for Hebrews

1. God speaks—in His Son!
2. The Son Incarnate
3. The Son Over His House
4. The Rest of Faith
5. His Priestly Appointment
6. Two Immutable Things
7. The Change of the Priesthood
8. The Change of the Covenant
9. The Better Sacrifice
10. The Seated Priest
11. The Hall of Fame, Heroes of Faith

12. Mt. Zion—*NOT* Sinai
13. The Christian's Altar

Application of the Message of Hebrews

God's Purpose—for us:

1. The full assurance of faith. Hebrews 10:22
2. Holding fast our confession of hope. Hebrews 10:23
3. The exercise of love. Hebrews 10:22–24

Hence, *5 warnings* in Hebrews:

1. *Pay attention*—don't drift—don't neglect so great a salvation. 2:1–3
2. *Hear His Voice*—don't harden your heart—don't disbelieve. 3:7–4:13
3. *Go on to maturity*—don't be a baby forever—don't stop short of receiving your full inheritance. Some have even missed salvation by not going on. 5:11–6:12
4. *Draw near to God* in the full assurance of faith—don't reject the person and work of Christ—apart from Him there is only judgment. 10:17–31
5. *Come to Jesus,* the Mediator of the new covenant. *Don't refuse Him who speaks.* The only alternative is the judgment of God. 12:18–29

For those who are in Christ this book is a message of assurance and security—because of the intercession of our *Great High Priest,* who ever lives to make intercession for us. Hebrews 7:25
*He appeared *once* to put away sin by the offering of Himself. Hebrews 9:26
*He appears *now* in the presence of God for us.
*He shall appear *again*—apart from the matter of sin—unto salvation (completing that which He has begun in us).
". . . *He is able to perfect completely those who come unto God by Him* . . ." Hebrews 7:25

For those who have *not* placed their faith in Christ, Hebrews warns of the peril of their position and exhorts to go on to "the full assurance of faith," by appropriating all that is available in Christ by God's grace.

Appendix E

The following diagrams illustrate some important interpretive premises we do well to heed as we seek to understand God's Word:

INTERPRETIVE PREMISES

Chart 1. Context

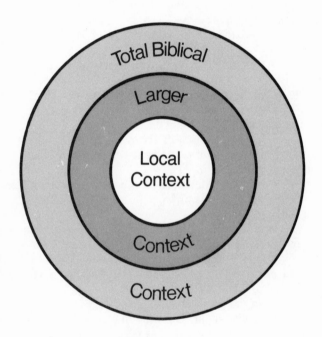

The relative weight we give either local or larger context will often determine our interpretive conclusion or opinion. Weigh all three: local, larger, and total biblical context carefully.

Chart 2. Setting

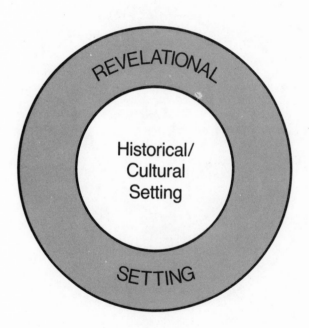

Though the historical/cultural setting is important, the overriding fact is that *the Bible is a revelation from God*. And God is not limited by history and culture. He had the last chapter in mind before the first was recorded. God transcends history.

Chart 3. Levels of Understanding

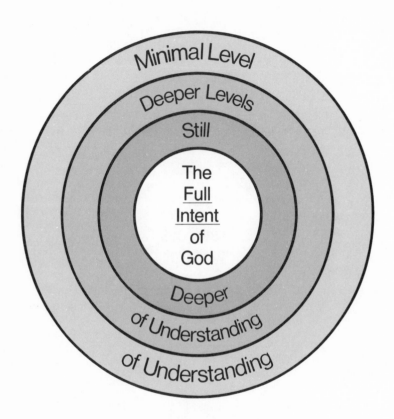

The full intent of meaning implanted by God in his revelation of truth is deeper than our understanding of his truth. It is doubtful if anyone fully understands all that God says in his Word. All of us will move to deeper levels of understanding as we grow. Our deeper understanding does not invalidate our previous minimal knowledge.

Conclusion: interpretive dogmatism is unwarranted; emotional defenses of our interpretive opinions are unprofitable. We need to grant that our Christian brother may have deeper understanding of the truth than we.